Data Protection Act 1998

CHAPTER 29

Explanatory Notes are available separately

GRAN*GIS* UK Publishing

Adapted and published by GRANGIS (Grand Register Library).
Online: www.grangis.com
E-mail: contact@grangis.com

In this version:
ISBN: 979-8-88559-015-0

Note: This is the original version (as it was originally enacted). Title, sub-title and the generated date is as marked on the pages.

Data Protection Act 1998

CHAPTER 29

DATA PROTECTION ACT 1998

PART I

PRELIMINARY

PART II

RIGHTS OF DATA SUBJECTS AND OTHERS

PART III

NOTIFICATION BY DATA CONTROLLERS

Data Protection Act 1998

1998 CHAPTER 29

An Act to make new provision for the regulation of the processing of information relating to individuals, including the obtaining, holding, use or disclosure of such information. [16th July 1998]

Be it enacted by the Queen's most Excellent Majesty, by and with the advice and consent of the Lords Spiritual and Temporal, and Commons, in this present Parliament assembled, and by the authority of the same, as follows:—

PART I

PRELIMINARY

1 Basic interpretative provisions

(1) In this Act, unless the context otherwise requires—

"data" means information which—

(a) is being processed by means of equipment operating automatically in response to instructions given for that purpose,

(b) is recorded with the intention that it should be processed by means of such equipment,

(c) is recorded as part of a relevant filing system or with the intention that it should form part of a relevant filing system, or

(d) does not fall within paragraph (a), (b) or (c) but forms part of an accessible record as defined by section 68;

"data controller" means, subject to subsection (4), a person who (either alone or jointly or in common with other persons) determines the purposes for which and the manner in which any personal data are, or are to be, processed;

"data processor", in relation to personal data, means any person (other than an employee of the data controller) who processes the data on behalf of the data controller;

"data subject" means an individual who is the subject of personal data;

"personal data" means data which relate to a living individual who can be identified—

(a) from those data, or

(b) from those data and other information which is in the possession of, or is likely to come into the possession of, the data controller,

and includes any expression of opinion about the individual and any indication of the intentions of the data controller or any other person in respect of the individual;

"processing", in relation to information or data, means obtaining, recording or holding the information or data or carrying out any operation or set of operations on the information or data, including—

(a) organisation, adaptation or alteration of the information or data,

(b) retrieval, consultation or use of the information or data,

(c) disclosure of the information or data by transmission, dissemination or otherwise making available, or

(d) alignment, combination, blocking, erasure or destruction of the information or data;

"relevant filing system" means any set of information relating to individuals to the extent that, although the information is not processed by means of equipment operating automatically in response to instructions given for that purpose, the set is structured, either by reference to individuals or by reference to criteria relating to individuals, in such a way that specific information relating to a particular individual is readily accessible.

(2) In this Act, unless the context otherwise requires—

(a) "obtaining" or "recording", in relation to personal data, includes obtaining or recording the information to be contained in the data, and

(b) "using" or "disclosing", in relation to personal data, includes using or disclosing the information contained in the data.

(3) In determining for the purposes of this Act whether any information is recorded with the intention—

(a) that it should be processed by means of equipment operating automatically in response to instructions given for that purpose, or

(b) that it should form part of a relevant filing system,

it is immaterial that it is intended to be so processed or to form part of such a system only after being transferred to a country or territory outside the European Economic Area.

(4) Where personal data are processed only for purposes for which they are required by or under any enactment to be processed, the person on whom the obligation to process the data is imposed by or under that enactment is for the purposes of this Act the data controller.

2 Sensitive personal data

In this Act "sensitive personal data" means personal data consisting of information as to—

(a) the racial or ethnic origin of the data subject,

(b) his political opinions,
(c) his religious beliefs or other beliefs of a similar nature,
(d) whether he is a member of a trade union (within the meaning of the Trade Union and Labour Relations (Consolidation) Act 1992),
(e) his physical or mental health or condition,
(f) his sexual life,
(g) the commission or alleged commission by him of any offence, or
(h) any proceedings for any offence committed or alleged to have been committed by him, the disposal of such proceedings or the sentence of any court in such proceedings.

3 The special purposes

In this Act "the special purposes" means any one or more of the following—
(a) the purposes of journalism,
(b) artistic purposes, and
(c) literary purposes.

4 The data protection principles

(1) References in this Act to the data protection principles are to the principles set out in Part I of Schedule 1.

(2) Those principles are to be interpreted in accordance with Part II of Schedule 1.

(3) Schedule 2 (which applies to all personal data) and Schedule 3 (which applies only to sensitive personal data) set out conditions applying for the purposes of the first principle; and Schedule 4 sets out cases in which the eighth principle does not apply.

(4) Subject to section 27(1), it shall be the duty of a data controller to comply with the data protection principles in relation to all personal data with respect to which he is the data controller.

5 Application of Act

(1) Except as otherwise provided by or under section 54, this Act applies to a data controller in respect of any data only if—
(a) the data controller is established in the United Kingdom and the data are processed in the context of that establishment, or
(b) the data controller is established neither in the United Kingdom nor in any other EEA State but uses equipment in the United Kingdom for processing the data otherwise than for the purposes of transit through the United Kingdom.

(2) A data controller falling within subsection (1)(b) must nominate for the purposes of this Act a representative established in the United Kingdom.

(3) For the purposes of subsections (1) and (2), each of the following is to be treated as established in the United Kingdom—
(a) an individual who is ordinarily resident in the United Kingdom,
(b) a body incorporated under the law of, or of any part of, the United Kingdom,

(c) a partnership or other unincorporated association formed under the law of any part of the United Kingdom, and

(d) any person who does not fall within paragraph (a), (b) or (c) but maintains in the United Kingdom—

(i) an office, branch or agency through which he carries on any activity, or

(ii) a regular practice;

and the reference to establishment in any other EEA State has a corresponding meaning.

6 The Commissioner and the Tribunal

(1) The office originally established by section 3(1)(a) of the Data Protection Act 1984 as the office of Data Protection Registrar shall continue to exist for the purposes of this Act but shall be known as the office of Data Protection Commissioner; and in this Act the Data Protection Commissioner is referred to as "the Commissioner".

(2) The Commissioner shall be appointed by Her Majesty by Letters Patent.

(3) For the purposes of this Act there shall continue to be a Data Protection Tribunal (in this Act referred to as "the Tribunal").

(4) The Tribunal shall consist of—

(a) a chairman appointed by the Lord Chancellor after consultation with the Lord Advocate,

(b) such number of deputy chairmen so appointed as the Lord Chancellor may determine, and

(c) such number of other members appointed by the Secretary of State as he may determine.

(5) The members of the Tribunal appointed under subsection (4)(a) and (b) shall be—

(a) persons who have a 7 year general qualification, within the meaning of section 71 of the Courts and Legal Services Act 1990,

(b) advocates or solicitors in Scotland of at least 7 years' standing, or

(c) members of the bar of Northern Ireland or solicitors of the Supreme Court of Northern Ireland of at least 7 years' standing.

(6) The members of the Tribunal appointed under subsection (4)(c) shall be—

(a) persons to represent the interests of data subjects, and

(b) persons to represent the interests of data controllers.

(7) Schedule 5 has effect in relation to the Commissioner and the Tribunal.

PART II

RIGHTS OF DATA SUBJECTS AND OTHERS

7 Right of access to personal data

(1) Subject to the following provisions of this section and to sections 8 and 9, an individual is entitled—

(a) to be informed by any data controller whether personal data of which that individual is the data subject are being processed by or on behalf of that data controller,

(b) if that is the case, to be given by the data controller a description of—

(i) the personal data of which that individual is the data subject,

(ii) the purposes for which they are being or are to be processed, and

(iii) the recipients or classes of recipients to whom they are or may be disclosed,

(c) to have communicated to him in an intelligible form—

(i) the information constituting any personal data of which that individual is the data subject, and

(ii) any information available to the data controller as to the source of those data, and

(d) where the processing by automatic means of personal data of which that individual is the data subject for the purpose of evaluating matters relating to him such as, for example, his performance at work, his creditworthiness, his reliability or his conduct, has constituted or is likely to constitute the sole basis for any decision significantly affecting him, to be informed by the data controller of the logic involved in that decision-taking.

(2) A data controller is not obliged to supply any information under subsection (1) unless he has received—

(a) a request in writing, and

(b) except in prescribed cases, such fee (not exceeding the prescribed maximum) as he may require.

(3) A data controller is not obliged to comply with a request under this section unless he is supplied with such information as he may reasonably require in order to satisfy himself as to the identity of the person making the request and to locate the information which that person seeks.

(4) Where a data controller cannot comply with the request without disclosing information relating to another individual who can be identified from that information, he is not obliged to comply with the request unless—

(a) the other individual has consented to the disclosure of the information to the person making the request, or

(b) it is reasonable in all the circumstances to comply with the request without the consent of the other individual.

(5) In subsection (4) the reference to information relating to another individual includes a reference to information identifying that individual as the source of the information sought by the request; and that subsection is not to be construed as excusing a data controller from communicating so much of the information sought by the request as can be communicated without disclosing the identity of the other individual concerned, whether by the omission of names or other identifying particulars or otherwise.

(6) In determining for the purposes of subsection (4)(b) whether it is reasonable in all the circumstances to comply with the request without the consent of the other individual concerned, regard shall be had, in particular, to—

(a) any duty of confidentiality owed to the other individual,

(b) any steps taken by the data controller with a view to seeking the consent of the other individual,

(c) whether the other individual is capable of giving consent, and

(d) any express refusal of consent by the other individual.

(7) An individual making a request under this section may, in such cases as may be prescribed, specify that his request is limited to personal data of any prescribed description.

(8) Subject to subsection (4), a data controller shall comply with a request under this section promptly and in any event before the end of the prescribed period beginning with the relevant day.

(9) If a court is satisfied on the application of any person who has made a request under the foregoing provisions of this section that the data controller in question has failed to comply with the request in contravention of those provisions, the court may order him to comply with the request.

(10) In this section—

"prescribed" means prescribed by the Secretary of State by regulations;

"the prescribed maximum" means such amount as may be prescribed;

"the prescribed period" means forty days or such other period as may be prescribed;

"the relevant day", in relation to a request under this section, means the day on which the data controller receives the request or, if later, the first day on which the data controller has both the required fee and the information referred to in subsection (3).

(11) Different amounts or periods may be prescribed under this section in relation to different cases.

8 Provisions supplementary to section 7

(1) The Secretary of State may by regulations provide that, in such cases as may be prescribed, a request for information under any provision of subsection (1) of section 7 is to be treated as extending also to information under other provisions of that subsection.

(2) The obligation imposed by section 7(1)(c)(i) must be complied with by supplying the data subject with a copy of the information in permanent form unless—

(a) the supply of such a copy is not possible or would involve disproportionate effort, or

(b) the data subject agrees otherwise;

and where any of the information referred to in section 7(1)(c)(i) is expressed in terms which are not intelligible without explanation the copy must be accompanied by an explanation of those terms.

(3) Where a data controller has previously complied with a request made under section 7 by an individual, the data controller is not obliged to comply with a subsequent identical or similar request under that section by that individual unless a reasonable interval has elapsed between compliance with the previous request and the making of the current request.

(4) In determining for the purposes of subsection (3) whether requests under section 7 are made at reasonable intervals, regard shall be had to the nature of the data, the purpose for which the data are processed and the frequency with which the data are altered.

(5) Section 7(1)(d) is not to be regarded as requiring the provision of information as to the logic involved in any decision-taking if, and to the extent that, the information constitutes a trade secret.

(6) The information to be supplied pursuant to a request under section 7 must be supplied by reference to the data in question at the time when the request is received, except that it may take account of any amendment or deletion made between that time and the time when the information is supplied, being an amendment or deletion that would have been made regardless of the receipt of the request.

(7) For the purposes of section 7(4) and (5) another individual can be identified from the information being disclosed if he can be identified from that information, or from that and any other information which, in the reasonable belief of the data controller, is likely to be in, or to come into, the possession of the data subject making the request.

9 Application of section 7 where data controller is credit reference agency

(1) Where the data controller is a credit reference agency, section 7 has effect subject to the provisions of this section.

(2) An individual making a request under section 7 may limit his request to personal data relevant to his financial standing, and shall be taken to have so limited his request unless the request shows a contrary intention.

(3) Where the data controller receives a request under section 7 in a case where personal data of which the individual making the request is the data subject are being processed by or on behalf of the data controller, the obligation to supply information under that section includes an obligation to give the individual making the request a statement, in such form as may be prescribed by the Secretary of State by regulations, of the individual's rights—

(a) under section 159 of the Consumer Credit Act 1974 , and

(b) to the extent required by the prescribed form, under this Act.

10 Right to prevent processing likely to cause damage or distress

(1) Subject to subsection (2), an individual is entitled at any time by notice in writing to a data controller to require the data controller at the end of such period as is reasonable in the circumstances to cease, or not to begin, processing, or processing for a specified purpose or in a specified manner, any personal data in respect of which he is the data subject, on the ground that, for specified reasons—

(a) the processing of those data or their processing for that purpose or in that manner is causing or is likely to cause substantial damage or substantial distress to him or to another, and

(b) that damage or distress is or would be unwarranted.

(2) Subsection (1) does not apply—

(a) in a case where any of the conditions in paragraphs 1 to 4 of Schedule 2 is met, or

(b) in such other cases as may be prescribed by the Secretary of State by order.

(3) The data controller must within twenty-one days of receiving a notice under subsection (1) ("the data subject notice") give the individual who gave it a written notice—

(a) stating that he has complied or intends to comply with the data subject notice, or

(b) stating his reasons for regarding the data subject notice as to any extent unjustified and the extent (if any) to which he has complied or intends to comply with it.

(4) If a court is satisfied, on the application of any person who has given a notice under subsection (1) which appears to the court to be justified (or to be justified to any extent), that the data controller in question has failed to comply with the notice, the court may order him to take such steps for complying with the notice (or for complying with it to that extent) as the court thinks fit.

(5) The failure by a data subject to exercise the right conferred by subsection (1) or section 11(1) does not affect any other right conferred on him by this Part.

11 Right to prevent processing for purposes of direct marketing

(1) An individual is entitled at any time by notice in writing to a data controller to require the data controller at the end of such period as is reasonable in the circumstances to cease, or not to begin, processing for the purposes of direct marketing personal data in respect of which he is the data subject.

(2) If the court is satisfied, on the application of any person who has given a notice under subsection (1), that the data controller has failed to comply with the notice, the court may order him to take such steps for complying with the notice as the court thinks fit.

(3) In this section "direct marketing" means the communication (by whatever means) of any advertising or marketing material which is directed to particular individuals.

12 Rights in relation to automated decision-taking

(1) An individual is entitled at any time, by notice in writing to any data controller, to require the data controller to ensure that no decision taken by or on behalf of the data controller which significantly affects that individual is based solely on the processing by automatic means of personal data in respect of which that individual is the data subject for the purpose of evaluating matters relating to him such as, for example, his performance at work, his creditworthiness, his reliability or his conduct.

(2) Where, in a case where no notice under subsection (1) has effect, a decision which significantly affects an individual is based solely on such processing as is mentioned in subsection (1)—

(a) the data controller must as soon as reasonably practicable notify the individual that the decision was taken on that basis, and

(b) the individual is entitled, within twenty-one days of receiving that notification from the data controller, by notice in writing to require the data controller to reconsider the decision or to take a new decision otherwise than on that basis.

(3) The data controller must, within twenty-one days of receiving a notice under subsection (2)(b) ("the data subject notice") give the individual a written notice specifying the steps that he intends to take to comply with the data subject notice.

(4) A notice under subsection (1) does not have effect in relation to an exempt decision; and nothing in subsection (2) applies to an exempt decision.

(5) In subsection (4) "exempt decision" means any decision—
  (a) in respect of which the condition in subsection (6) and the condition in subsection (7) are met, or
  (b) which is made in such other circumstances as may be prescribed by the Secretary of State by order.

(6) The condition in this subsection is that the decision—
  (a) is taken in the course of steps taken—
    (i) for the purpose of considering whether to enter into a contract with the data subject,
    (ii) with a view to entering into such a contract, or
    (iii) in the course of performing such a contract, or
  (b) is authorised or required by or under any enactment.

(7) The condition in this subsection is that either—
  (a) the effect of the decision is to grant a request of the data subject, or
  (b) steps have been taken to safeguard the legitimate interests of the data subject (for example, by allowing him to make representations).

(8) If a court is satisfied on the application of a data subject that a person taking a decision in respect of him ("the responsible person") has failed to comply with subsection (1) or (2)(b), the court may order the responsible person to reconsider the decision, or to take a new decision which is not based solely on such processing as is mentioned in subsection (1).

(9) An order under subsection (8) shall not affect the rights of any person other than the data subject and the responsible person.

13 Compensation for failure to comply with certain requirements

(1) An individual who suffers damage by reason of any contravention by a data controller of any of the requirements of this Act is entitled to compensation from the data controller for that damage.

(2) An individual who suffers distress by reason of any contravention by a data controller of any of the requirements of this Act is entitled to compensation from the data controller for that distress if—
  (a) the individual also suffers damage by reason of the contravention, or
  (b) the contravention relates to the processing of personal data for the special purposes.

(3) In proceedings brought against a person by virtue of this section it is a defence to prove that he had taken such care as in all the circumstances was reasonably required to comply with the requirement concerned.

14 Rectification, blocking, erasure and destruction

(1) If a court is satisfied on the application of a data subject that personal data of which the applicant is the subject are inaccurate, the court may order the data controller to rectify, block, erase or destroy those data and any other personal data in respect of which he is the data controller and which contain an expression of opinion which appears to the court to be based on the inaccurate data.

(2) Subsection (1) applies whether or not the data accurately record information received or obtained by the data controller from the data subject or a third party but where the data accurately record such information, then—

(a) if the requirements mentioned in paragraph 7 of Part II of Schedule 1 have been complied with, the court may, instead of making an order under subsection (1), make an order requiring the data to be supplemented by such statement of the true facts relating to the matters dealt with by the data as the court may approve, and

(b) if all or any of those requirements have not been complied with, the court may, instead of making an order under that subsection, make such order as it thinks fit for securing compliance with those requirements with or without a further order requiring the data to be supplemented by such a statement as is mentioned in paragraph (a).

(3) Where the court—

(a) makes an order under subsection (1), or

(b) is satisfied on the application of a data subject that personal data of which he was the data subject and which have been rectified, blocked, erased or destroyed were inaccurate,

it may, where it considers it reasonably practicable, order the data controller to notify third parties to whom the data have been disclosed of the rectification, blocking, erasure or destruction.

(4) If a court is satisfied on the application of a data subject—

(a) that he has suffered damage by reason of any contravention by a data controller of any of the requirements of this Act in respect of any personal data, in circumstances entitling him to compensation under section 13, and

(b) that there is a substantial risk of further contravention in respect of those data in such circumstances,

the court may order the rectification, blocking, erasure or destruction of any of those data.

(5) Where the court makes an order under subsection (4) it may, where it considers it reasonably practicable, order the data controller to notify third parties to whom the data have been disclosed of the rectification, blocking, erasure or destruction.

(6) In determining whether it is reasonably practicable to require such notification as is mentioned in subsection (3) or (5) the court shall have regard, in particular, to the number of persons who would have to be notified.

15 Jurisdiction and procedure

(1) The jurisdiction conferred by sections 7 to 14 is exercisable by the High Court or a county court or, in Scotland, by the Court of Session or the sheriff.

(2) For the purpose of determining any question whether an applicant under subsection (9) of section 7 is entitled to the information which he seeks (including any question whether any relevant data are exempt from that section by virtue of Part IV) a court may require the information constituting any data processed by or on behalf of the data controller and any information as to the logic involved in any decision-taking as mentioned in section 7(1)(d) to be made available for its own inspection but shall not, pending the determination of that question in the applicant's favour, require the

information sought by the applicant to be disclosed to him or his representatives whether by discovery (or, in Scotland, recovery) or otherwise.

PART III

NOTIFICATION BY DATA CONTROLLERS

16 Preliminary

(1) In this Part "the registrable particulars", in relation to a data controller, means—

(a) his name and address,

(b) if he has nominated a representative for the purposes of this Act, the name and address of the representative,

(c) a description of the personal data being or to be processed by or on behalf of the data controller and of the category or categories of data subject to which they relate,

(d) a description of the purpose or purposes for which the data are being or are to be processed,

(e) a description of any recipient or recipients to whom the data controller intends or may wish to disclose the data,

(f) the names, or a description of, any countries or territories outside the European Economic Area to which the data controller directly or indirectly transfers, or intends or may wish directly or indirectly to transfer, the data, and

(g) in any case where—

(i) personal data are being, or are intended to be, processed in circumstances in which the prohibition in subsection (1) of section 17 is excluded by subsection (2) or (3) of that section, and

(ii) the notification does not extend to those data,

a statement of that fact.

(2) In this Part—

"fees regulations" means regulations made by the Secretary of State under section 18(5) or 19(4) or (7);

"notification regulations" means regulations made by the Secretary of State under the other provisions of this Part;

"prescribed", except where used in relation to fees regulations, means prescribed by notification regulations.

(3) For the purposes of this Part, so far as it relates to the addresses of data controllers—

(a) the address of a registered company is that of its registered office, and

(b) the address of a person (other than a registered company) carrying on a business is that of his principal place of business in the United Kingdom.

17 Prohibition on processing without registration

(1) Subject to the following provisions of this section, personal data must not be processed unless an entry in respect of the data controller is included in the register maintained by the Commissioner under section 19 (or is treated by notification regulations made by virtue of section 19(3) as being so included).

(2) Except where the processing is assessable processing for the purposes of section 22, subsection (1) does not apply in relation to personal data consisting of information which falls neither within paragraph (a) of the definition of "data" in section 1(1) nor within paragraph (b) of that definition.

(3) If it appears to the Secretary of State that processing of a particular description is unlikely to prejudice the rights and freedoms of data subjects, notification regulations may provide that, in such cases as may be prescribed, subsection (1) is not to apply in relation to processing of that description.

(4) Subsection (1) does not apply in relation to any processing whose sole purpose is the maintenance of a public register.

18 Notification by data controllers

(1) Any data controller who wishes to be included in the register maintained under section 19 shall give a notification to the Commissioner under this section.

(2) A notification under this section must specify in accordance with notification regulations—

(a) the registrable particulars, and

(b) a general description of measures to be taken for the purpose of complying with the seventh data protection principle.

(3) Notification regulations made by virtue of subsection (2) may provide for the determination by the Commissioner, in accordance with any requirements of the regulations, of the form in which the registrable particulars and the description mentioned in subsection (2)(b) are to be specified, including in particular the detail required for the purposes of section 16(1)(c), (d), (e) and (f) and subsection (2)(b).

(4) Notification regulations may make provision as to the giving of notification—

(a) by partnerships, or

(b) in other cases where two or more persons are the data controllers in respect of any personal data.

(5) The notification must be accompanied by such fee as may be prescribed by fees regulations.

(6) Notification regulations may provide for any fee paid under subsection (5) or section 19(4) to be refunded in prescribed circumstances.

19 Register of notifications

(1) The Commissioner shall—

(a) maintain a register of persons who have given notification under section 18, and

(b) make an entry in the register in pursuance of each notification received by him under that section from a person in respect of whom no entry as data controller was for the time being included in the register.

(2) Each entry in the register shall consist of—

(a) the registrable particulars notified under section 18 or, as the case requires, those particulars as amended in pursuance of section 20(4), and

(b) such other information as the Commissioner may be authorised or required by notification regulations to include in the register.

(3) Notification regulations may make provision as to the time as from which any entry in respect of a data controller is to be treated for the purposes of section 17 as having been made in the register.

(4) No entry shall be retained in the register for more than the relevant time except on payment of such fee as may be prescribed by fees regulations.

(5) In subsection (4) "the relevant time" means twelve months or such other period as may be prescribed by notification regulations; and different periods may be prescribed in relation to different cases.

(6) The Commissioner—

(a) shall provide facilities for making the information contained in the entries in the register available for inspection (in visible and legible form) by members of the public at all reasonable hours and free of charge, and

(b) may provide such other facilities for making the information contained in those entries available to the public free of charge as he considers appropriate.

(7) The Commissioner shall, on payment of such fee, if any, as may be prescribed by fees regulations, supply any member of the public with a duly certified copy in writing of the particulars contained in any entry made in the register.

20 Duty to notify changes

(1) For the purpose specified in subsection (2), notification regulations shall include provision imposing on every person in respect of whom an entry as a data controller is for the time being included in the register maintained under section 19 a duty to notify to the Commissioner, in such circumstances and at such time or times and in such form as may be prescribed, such matters relating to the registrable particulars and measures taken as mentioned in section 18(2)(b) as may be prescribed.

(2) The purpose referred to in subsection (1) is that of ensuring, so far as practicable, that at any time—

(a) the entries in the register maintained under section 19 contain current names and addresses and describe the current practice or intentions of the data controller with respect to the processing of personal data, and

(b) the Commissioner is provided with a general description of measures currently being taken as mentioned in section 18(2)(b).

(3) Subsection (3) of section 18 has effect in relation to notification regulations made by virtue of subsection (1) as it has effect in relation to notification regulations made by virtue of subsection (2) of that section.

(4) On receiving any notification under notification regulations made by virtue of subsection (1), the Commissioner shall make such amendments of the relevant entry in the register maintained under section 19 as are necessary to take account of the notification.

21 Offences

(1) If section 17(1) is contravened, the data controller is guilty of an offence.

(2) Any person who fails to comply with the duty imposed by notification regulations made by virtue of section 20(1) is guilty of an offence.

(3) It shall be a defence for a person charged with an offence under subsection (2) to show that he exercised all due diligence to comply with the duty.

22 Preliminary assessment by Commissioner

(1) In this section "assessable processing" means processing which is of a description specified in an order made by the Secretary of State as appearing to him to be particularly likely—

(a) to cause substantial damage or substantial distress to data subjects, or

(b) otherwise significantly to prejudice the rights and freedoms of data subjects.

(2) On receiving notification from any data controller under section 18 or under notification regulations made by virtue of section 20 the Commissioner shall consider—

(a) whether any of the processing to which the notification relates is assessable processing, and

(b) if so, whether the assessable processing is likely to comply with the provisions of this Act.

(3) Subject to subsection (4), the Commissioner shall, within the period of twenty-eight days beginning with the day on which he receives a notification which relates to assessable processing, give a notice to the data controller stating the extent to which the Commissioner is of the opinion that the processing is likely or unlikely to comply with the provisions of this Act.

(4) Before the end of the period referred to in subsection (3) the Commissioner may, by reason of special circumstances, extend that period on one occasion only by notice to the data controller by such further period not exceeding fourteen days as the Commissioner may specify in the notice.

(5) No assessable processing in respect of which a notification has been given to the Commissioner as mentioned in subsection (2) shall be carried on unless either—

(a) the period of twenty-eight days beginning with the day on which the notification is received by the Commissioner (or, in a case falling within subsection (4), that period as extended under that subsection) has elapsed, or

(b) before the end of that period (or that period as so extended) the data controller has received a notice from the Commissioner under subsection (3) in respect of the processing.

(6) Where subsection (5) is contravened, the data controller is guilty of an offence.

(7) The Secretary of State may by order amend subsections (3), (4) and (5) by substituting for the number of days for the time being specified there a different number specified in the order.

23 Power to make provision for appointment of data protection supervisors

(1) The Secretary of State may by order—

(a) make provision under which a data controller may appoint a person to act as a data protection supervisor responsible in particular for monitoring in an independent manner the data controller's compliance with the provisions of this Act, and

(b) provide that, in relation to any data controller who has appointed a data protection supervisor in accordance with the provisions of the order and who complies with such conditions as may be specified in the order, the provisions of this Part are to have effect subject to such exemptions or other modifications as may be specified in the order.

(2) An order under this section may—

(a) impose duties on data protection supervisors in relation to the Commissioner, and

(b) confer functions on the Commissioner in relation to data protection supervisors.

24 Duty of certain data controllers to make certain information available

(1) Subject to subsection (3), where personal data are processed in a case where—

(a) by virtue of subsection (2) or (3) of section 17, subsection (1) of that section does not apply to the processing, and

(b) the data controller has not notified the relevant particulars in respect of that processing under section 18,

the data controller must, within twenty-one days of receiving a written request from any person, make the relevant particulars available to that person in writing free of charge.

(2) In this section "the relevant particulars" means the particulars referred to in paragraphs (a) to (f) of section 16(1).

(3) This section has effect subject to any exemption conferred for the purposes of this section by notification regulations.

(4) Any data controller who fails to comply with the duty imposed by subsection (1) is guilty of an offence.

(5) It shall be a defence for a person charged with an offence under subsection (4) to show that he exercised all due diligence to comply with the duty.

25 Functions of Commissioner in relation to making of notification regulations

(1) As soon as practicable after the passing of this Act, the Commissioner shall submit to the Secretary of State proposals as to the provisions to be included in the first notification regulations.

(2) The Commissioner shall keep under review the working of notification regulations and may from time to time submit to the Secretary of State proposals as to amendments to be made to the regulations.

(3) The Secretary of State may from time to time require the Commissioner to consider any matter relating to notification regulations and to submit to him proposals as to amendments to be made to the regulations in connection with that matter.

(4) Before making any notification regulations, the Secretary of State shall—

(a) consider any proposals made to him by the Commissioner under subsection (1), (2) or (3), and

(b) consult the Commissioner.

26 Fees regulations

(1) Fees regulations prescribing fees for the purposes of any provision of this Part may provide for different fees to be payable in different cases.

(2) In making any fees regulations, the Secretary of State shall have regard to the desirability of securing that the fees payable to the Commissioner are sufficient to offset—

(a) the expenses incurred by the Commissioner and the Tribunal in discharging their functions and any expenses of the Secretary of State in respect of the Commissioner or the Tribunal, and

(b) to the extent that the Secretary of State considers appropriate—

(i) any deficit previously incurred (whether before or after the passing of this Act) in respect of the expenses mentioned in paragraph (a), and

(ii) expenses incurred or to be incurred by the Secretary of State in respect of the inclusion of any officers or staff of the Commissioner in any scheme under section 1 of the Superannuation Act 1972.

PART IV

EXEMPTIONS

27 Preliminary

(1) References in any of the data protection principles or any provision of Parts II and III to personal data or to the processing of personal data do not include references to data or processing which by virtue of this Part are exempt from that principle or other provision.

(2) In this Part "the subject information provisions" means—

(a) the first data protection principle to the extent to which it requires compliance with paragraph 2 of Part II of Schedule 1, and

(b) section 7.

(3) In this Part "the non-disclosure provisions" means the provisions specified in subsection (4) to the extent to which they are inconsistent with the disclosure in question.

(4) The provisions referred to in subsection (3) are—

(a) the first data protection principle, except to the extent to which it requires compliance with the conditions in Schedules 2 and 3,

(b) the second, third, fourth and fifth data protection principles, and

(c) sections 10 and 14(1) to (3).

(5) Except as provided by this Part, the subject information provisions shall have effect notwithstanding any enactment or rule of law prohibiting or restricting the disclosure, or authorising the withholding, of information.

28 National security

(1) Personal data are exempt from any of the provisions of—

(a) the data protection principles,

(b) Parts II, III and V, and

(c) section 55,

if the exemption from that provision is required for the purpose of safeguarding national security.

(2) Subject to subsection (4), a certificate signed by a Minister of the Crown certifying that exemption from all or any of the provisions mentioned in subsection (1) is or at any time was required for the purpose there mentioned in respect of any personal data shall be conclusive evidence of that fact.

(3) A certificate under subsection (2) may identify the personal data to which it applies by means of a general description and may be expressed to have prospective effect.

(4) Any person directly affected by the issuing of a certificate under subsection (2) may appeal to the Tribunal against the certificate.

(5) If on an appeal under subsection (4), the Tribunal finds that, applying the principles applied by the court on an application for judicial review, the Minister did not have reasonable grounds for issuing the certificate, the Tribunal may allow the appeal and quash the certificate.

(6) Where in any proceedings under or by virtue of this Act it is claimed by a data controller that a certificate under subsection (2) which identifies the personal data to which it applies by means of a general description applies to any personal data, any other party to the proceedings may appeal to the Tribunal on the ground that the certificate does not apply to the personal data in question and, subject to any determination under subsection (7), the certificate shall be conclusively presumed so to apply.

(7) On any appeal under subsection (6), the Tribunal may determine that the certificate does not so apply.

(8) A document purporting to be a certificate under subsection (2) shall be received in evidence and deemed to be such a certificate unless the contrary is proved.

(9) A document which purports to be certified by or on behalf of a Minister of the Crown as a true copy of a certificate issued by that Minister under subsection (2) shall in any legal proceedings be evidence (or, in Scotland, sufficient evidence) of that certificate.

(10) The power conferred by subsection (2) on a Minister of the Crown shall not be exercisable except by a Minister who is a member of the Cabinet or by the Attorney General or the Lord Advocate.

(11) No power conferred by any provision of Part V may be exercised in relation to personal data which by virtue of this section are exempt from that provision.

(12) Schedule 6 shall have effect in relation to appeals under subsection (4) or (6) and the proceedings of the Tribunal in respect of any such appeal.

29 Crime and taxation

(1) Personal data processed for any of the following purposes—

(a) the prevention or detection of crime,
(b) the apprehension or prosecution of offenders, or
(c) the assessment or collection of any tax or duty or of any imposition of a similar nature,

are exempt from the first data protection principle (except to the extent to which it requires compliance with the conditions in Schedules 2 and 3) and section 7 in any case to the extent to which the application of those provisions to the data would be likely to prejudice any of the matters mentioned in this subsection.

(2) Personal data which—

(a) are processed for the purpose of discharging statutory functions, and
(b) consist of information obtained for such a purpose from a person who had it in his possession for any of the purposes mentioned in subsection (1),

are exempt from the subject information provisions to the same extent as personal data processed for any of the purposes mentioned in that subsection.

(3) Personal data are exempt from the non-disclosure provisions in any case in which—

(a) the disclosure is for any of the purposes mentioned in subsection (1), and
(b) the application of those provisions in relation to the disclosure would be likely to prejudice any of the matters mentioned in that subsection.

(4) Personal data in respect of which the data controller is a relevant authority and which—

(a) consist of a classification applied to the data subject as part of a system of risk assessment which is operated by that authority for either of the following purposes—
   (i) the assessment or collection of any tax or duty or any imposition of a similar nature, or
   (ii) the prevention or detection of crime, or apprehension or prosecution of offenders, where the offence concerned involves any unlawful claim for any payment out of, or any unlawful application of, public funds, and
(b) are processed for either of those purposes,

are exempt from section 7 to the extent to which the exemption is required in the interests of the operation of the system.

(5) In subsection (4)—

"public funds" includes funds provided by any Community institution;

"relevant authority" means—

(a) a government department,
(b) a local authority, or
(c) any other authority administering housing benefit or council tax benefit.

30 Health, education and social work

(1) The Secretary of State may by order exempt from the subject information provisions, or modify those provisions in relation to, personal data consisting of information as to the physical or mental health or condition of the data subject.

(2) The Secretary of State may by order exempt from the subject information provisions, or modify those provisions in relation to—

(a) personal data in respect of which the data controller is the proprietor of, or a teacher at, a school, and which consist of information relating to persons who are or have been pupils at the school, or

(b) personal data in respect of which the data controller is an education authority in Scotland, and which consist of information relating to persons who are receiving, or have received, further education provided by the authority.

(3) The Secretary of State may by order exempt from the subject information provisions, or modify those provisions in relation to, personal data of such other descriptions as may be specified in the order, being information—

(a) processed by government departments or local authorities or by voluntary organisations or other bodies designated by or under the order, and

(b) appearing to him to be processed in the course of, or for the purposes of, carrying out social work in relation to the data subject or other individuals;

but the Secretary of State shall not under this subsection confer any exemption or make any modification except so far as he considers that the application to the data of those provisions (or of those provisions without modification) would be likely to prejudice the carrying out of social work.

(4) An order under this section may make different provision in relation to data consisting of information of different descriptions.

(5) In this section—

"education authority" and "further education" have the same meaning as in the Education (Scotland) Act 1980 ("the 1980 Act"), and

"proprietor"—

(a) in relation to a school in England or Wales, has the same meaning as in the Education Act 1996,

(b) in relation to a school in Scotland, means—

(c) in the case of a self-governing school, the board of management within the meaning of the Self-Governing Schools etc. (Scotland) Act 1989,

(ii) in the case of an independent school, the proprietor within the meaning of the 1980 Act,

(iii) in the case of a grant-aided school, the managers within the meaning of the 1980 Act, and

(iv) in the case of a public school, the education authority within the meaning of the 1980 Act, and

(g) in relation to a school in Northern Ireland, has the same meaning as in the Education and Libraries (Northern Ireland) Order 1986 and includes, in the case of a controlled school, the Board of Governors of the school.

31 Regulatory activity

(1) Personal data processed for the purposes of discharging functions to which this subsection applies are exempt from the subject information provisions in any case to the extent to which the application of those provisions to the data would be likely to prejudice the proper discharge of those functions.

(2) Subsection (1) applies to any relevant function which is designed—

(a) for protecting members of the public against—

(i) financial loss due to dishonesty, malpractice or other seriously improper conduct by, or the unfitness or incompetence of, persons concerned in the provision of banking, insurance, investment or other financial services or in the management of bodies corporate,

(ii) financial loss due to the conduct of discharged or undischarged bankrupts, or

(iii) dishonesty, malpractice or other seriously improper conduct by, or the unfitness or incompetence of, persons authorised to carry on any profession or other activity,

(b) for protecting charities against misconduct or mismanagement (whether by trustees or other persons) in their administration,

(c) for protecting the property of charities from loss or misapplication,

(d) for the recovery of the property of charities,

(e) for securing the health, safety and welfare of persons at work, or

(f) for protecting persons other than persons at work against risk to health or safety arising out of or in connection with the actions of persons at work.

(3) In subsection (2) "relevant function" means—

(a) any function conferred on any person by or under any enactment,

(b) any function of the Crown, a Minister of the Crown or a government department, or

(c) any other function which is of a public nature and is exercised in the public interest.

(4) Personal data processed for the purpose of discharging any function which—

(a) is conferred by or under any enactment on—

(i) the Parliamentary Commissioner for Administration,

(ii) the Commission for Local Administration in England, the Commission for Local Administration in Wales or the Commissioner for Local Administration in Scotland,

(iii) the Health Service Commissioner for England, the Health Service Commissioner for Wales or the Health Service Commissioner for Scotland,

(iv) the Welsh Administration Ombudsman,

(v) the Assembly Ombudsman for Northern Ireland, or

(vi) the Northern Ireland Commissioner for Complaints, and

(b) is designed for protecting members of the public against—

(i) maladministration by public bodies,

(ii) failures in services provided by public bodies, or

(iii) a failure of a public body to provide a service which it was a function of the body to provide,

are exempt from the subject information provisions in any case to the extent to which the application of those provisions to the data would be likely to prejudice the proper discharge of that function.

(5) Personal data processed for the purpose of discharging any function which—

(a) is conferred by or under any enactment on the Director General of Fair Trading, and

(b) is designed—

(i) for protecting members of the public against conduct which may adversely affect their interests by persons carrying on a business,

(ii) for regulating agreements or conduct which have as their object or effect the prevention, restriction or distortion of competition in connection with any commercial activity, or

(iii) for regulating conduct on the part of one or more undertakings which amounts to the abuse of a dominant position in a market,

are exempt from the subject information provisions in any case to the extent to which the application of those provisions to the data would be likely to prejudice the proper discharge of that function.

32 Journalism, literature and art

(1) Personal data which are processed only for the special purposes are exempt from any provision to which this subsection relates if—

(a) the processing is undertaken with a view to the publication by any person of any journalistic, literary or artistic material,

(b) the data controller reasonably believes that, having regard in particular to the special importance of the public interest in freedom of expression, publication would be in the public interest, and

(c) the data controller reasonably believes that, in all the circumstances, compliance with that provision is incompatible with the special purposes.

(2) Subsection (1) relates to the provisions of—

(a) the data protection principles except the seventh data protection principle,

(b) section 7,

(c) section 10,

(d) section 12, and

(e) section 14(1) to (3).

(3) In considering for the purposes of subsection (1)(b) whether the belief of a data controller that publication would be in the public interest was or is a reasonable one, regard may be had to his compliance with any code of practice which—

(a) is relevant to the publication in question, and

(b) is designated by the Secretary of State by order for the purposes of this subsection.

(4) Where at any time ("the relevant time") in any proceedings against a data controller under section 7(9), 10(4), 12(8) or 14 or by virtue of section 13 the data controller claims, or it appears to the court, that any personal data to which the proceedings relate are being processed—

(a) only for the special purposes, and

(b) with a view to the publication by any person of any journalistic, literary or artistic material which, at the time twenty-four hours immediately before the relevant time, had not previously been published by the data controller,

the court shall stay the proceedings until either of the conditions in subsection (5) is met.

(5) Those conditions are—

(a) that a determination of the Commissioner under section 45 with respect to the data in question takes effect, or

(b) in a case where the proceedings were stayed on the making of a claim, that the claim is withdrawn.

(6) For the purposes of this Act "publish", in relation to journalistic, literary or artistic material, means make available to the public or any section of the public.

33 Research, history and statistics

(1) In this section—

"research purposes" includes statistical or historical purposes;

"the relevant conditions", in relation to any processing of personal data, means the conditions—

(a) that the data are not processed to support measures or decisions with respect to particular individuals, and

(b) that the data are not processed in such a way that substantial damage or substantial distress is, or is likely to be, caused to any data subject.

(2) For the purposes of the second data protection principle, the further processing of personal data only for research purposes in compliance with the relevant conditions is not to be regarded as incompatible with the purposes for which they were obtained.

(3) Personal data which are processed only for research purposes in compliance with the relevant conditions may, notwithstanding the fifth data protection principle, be kept indefinitely.

(4) Personal data which are processed only for research purposes are exempt from section 7 if—

(a) they are processed in compliance with the relevant conditions, and

(b) the results of the research or any resulting statistics are not made available in a form which identifies data subjects or any of them.

(5) For the purposes of subsections (2) to (4) personal data are not to be treated as processed otherwise than for research purposes merely because the data are disclosed—

(a) to any person, for research purposes only,

(b) to the data subject or a person acting on his behalf,

(c) at the request, or with the consent, of the data subject or a person acting on his behalf, or

(d) in circumstances in which the person making the disclosure has reasonable grounds for believing that the disclosure falls within paragraph (a), (b) or (c).

34 Information available to the public by or under enactment

Personal data are exempt from—

(a) the subject information provisions,

(b) the fourth data protection principle and section 14(1) to (3), and

(c) the non-disclosure provisions,

if the data consist of information which the data controller is obliged by or under any enactment to make available to the public, whether by publishing it, by making it available for inspection, or otherwise and whether gratuitously or on payment of a fee.

35 Disclosures required by law or made in connection with legal proceedings etc

(1) Personal data are exempt from the non-disclosure provisions where the disclosure is required by or under any enactment, by any rule of law or by the order of a court.

(2) Personal data are exempt from the non-disclosure provisions where the disclosure is necessary—

(a) for the purpose of, or in connection with, any legal proceedings (including prospective legal proceedings), or

(b) for the purpose of obtaining legal advice,

or is otherwise necessary for the purposes of establishing, exercising or defending legal rights.

36 Domestic purposes

Personal data processed by an individual only for the purposes of that individual's personal, family or household affairs (including recreational purposes) are exempt from the data protection principles and the provisions of Parts II and III.

37 Miscellaneous exemptions

Schedule 7 (which confers further miscellaneous exemptions) has effect.

38 Powers to make further exemptions by order

(1) The Secretary of State may by order exempt from the subject information provisions personal data consisting of information the disclosure of which is prohibited or restricted by or under any enactment if and to the extent that he considers it necessary for the safeguarding of the interests of the data subject or the rights and freedoms of any other individual that the prohibition or restriction ought to prevail over those provisions.

(2) The Secretary of State may by order exempt from the non-disclosure provisions any disclosures of personal data made in circumstances specified in the order, if he considers the exemption is necessary for the safeguarding of the interests of the data subject or the rights and freedoms of any other individual.

39 Transitional relief

Schedule 8 (which confers transitional exemptions) has effect.

PART V

ENFORCEMENT

40 Enforcement notices

(1) If the Commissioner is satisfied that a data controller has contravened or is contravening any of the data protection principles, the Commissioner may serve him with a notice (in this Act referred to as "an enforcement notice") requiring him, for

complying with the principle or principles in question, to do either or both of the following—

(a) to take within such time as may be specified in the notice, or to refrain from taking after such time as may be so specified, such steps as are so specified, or

(b) to refrain from processing any personal data, or any personal data of a description specified in the notice, or to refrain from processing them for a purpose so specified or in a manner so specified, after such time as may be so specified.

(2) In deciding whether to serve an enforcement notice, the Commissioner shall consider whether the contravention has caused or is likely to cause any person damage or distress.

(3) An enforcement notice in respect of a contravention of the fourth data protection principle which requires the data controller to rectify, block, erase or destroy any inaccurate data may also require the data controller to rectify, block, erase or destroy any other data held by him and containing an expression of opinion which appears to the Commissioner to be based on the inaccurate data.

(4) An enforcement notice in respect of a contravention of the fourth data protection principle, in the case of data which accurately record information received or obtained by the data controller from the data subject or a third party, may require the data controller either—

(a) to rectify, block, erase or destroy any inaccurate data and any other data held by him and containing an expression of opinion as mentioned in subsection (3), or

(b) to take such steps as are specified in the notice for securing compliance with the requirements specified in paragraph 7 of Part II of Schedule 1 and, if the Commissioner thinks fit, for supplementing the data with such statement of the true facts relating to the matters dealt with by the data as the Commissioner may approve.

(5) Where—

(a) an enforcement notice requires the data controller to rectify, block, erase or destroy any personal data, or

(b) the Commissioner is satisfied that personal data which have been rectified, blocked, erased or destroyed had been processed in contravention of any of the data protection principles,

an enforcement notice may, if reasonably practicable, require the data controller to notify third parties to whom the data have been disclosed of the rectification, blocking, erasure or destruction; and in determining whether it is reasonably practicable to require such notification regard shall be had, in particular, to the number of persons who would have to be notified.

(6) An enforcement notice must contain—

(a) a statement of the data protection principle or principles which the Commissioner is satisfied have been or are being contravened and his reasons for reaching that conclusion, and

(b) particulars of the rights of appeal conferred by section 48.

(7) Subject to subsection (8), an enforcement notice must not require any of the provisions of the notice to be complied with before the end of the period within which an appeal

can be brought against the notice and, if such an appeal is brought, the notice need not be complied with pending the determination or withdrawal of the appeal.

(8) If by reason of special circumstances the Commissioner considers that an enforcement notice should be complied with as a matter of urgency he may include in the notice a statement to that effect and a statement of his reasons for reaching that conclusion; and in that event subsection (7) shall not apply but the notice must not require the provisions of the notice to be complied with before the end of the period of seven days beginning with the day on which the notice is served.

(9) Notification regulations (as defined by section 16(2)) may make provision as to the effect of the service of an enforcement notice on any entry in the register maintained under section 19 which relates to the person on whom the notice is served.

(10) This section has effect subject to section 46(1).

41 Cancellation of enforcement notice

(1) If the Commissioner considers that all or any of the provisions of an enforcement notice need not be complied with in order to ensure compliance with the data protection principle or principles to which it relates, he may cancel or vary the notice by written notice to the person on whom it was served.

(2) A person on whom an enforcement notice has been served may, at any time after the expiry of the period during which an appeal can be brought against that notice, apply in writing to the Commissioner for the cancellation or variation of that notice on the ground that, by reason of a change of circumstances, all or any of the provisions of that notice need not be complied with in order to ensure compliance with the data protection principle or principles to which that notice relates.

42 Request for assessment

(1) A request may be made to the Commissioner by or on behalf of any person who is, or believes himself to be, directly affected by any processing of personal data for an assessment as to whether it is likely or unlikely that the processing has been or is being carried out in compliance with the provisions of this Act.

(2) On receiving a request under this section, the Commissioner shall make an assessment in such manner as appears to him to be appropriate, unless he has not been supplied with such information as he may reasonably require in order to—

(a) satisfy himself as to the identity of the person making the request, and
(b) enable him to identify the processing in question.

(3) The matters to which the Commissioner may have regard in determining in what manner it is appropriate to make an assessment include—

(a) the extent to which the request appears to him to raise a matter of substance,
(b) any undue delay in making the request, and
(c) whether or not the person making the request is entitled to make an application under section 7 in respect of the personal data in question.

(4) Where the Commissioner has received a request under this section he shall notify the person who made the request—

(a) whether he has made an assessment as a result of the request, and

(b) to the extent that he considers appropriate, having regard in particular to any exemption from section 7 applying in relation to the personal data concerned, of any view formed or action taken as a result of the request.

43 Information notices

(1) If the Commissioner—

(a) has received a request under section 42 in respect of any processing of personal data, or

(b) reasonably requires any information for the purpose of determining whether the data controller has complied or is complying with the data protection principles,

he may serve the data controller with a notice (in this Act referred to as "an information notice") requiring the data controller, within such time as is specified in the notice, to furnish the Commissioner, in such form as may be so specified, with such information relating to the request or to compliance with the principles as is so specified.

(2) An information notice must contain—

(a) in a case falling within subsection (1)(a), a statement that the Commissioner has received a request under section 42 in relation to the specified processing, or

(b) in a case falling within subsection (1)(b), a statement that the Commissioner regards the specified information as relevant for the purpose of determining whether the data controller has complied, or is complying, with the data protection principles and his reasons for regarding it as relevant for that purpose.

(3) An information notice must also contain particulars of the rights of appeal conferred by section 48.

(4) Subject to subsection (5), the time specified in an information notice shall not expire before the end of the period within which an appeal can be brought against the notice and, if such an appeal is brought, the information need not be furnished pending the determination or withdrawal of the appeal.

(5) If by reason of special circumstances the Commissioner considers that the information is required as a matter of urgency, he may include in the notice a statement to that effect and a statement of his reasons for reaching that conclusion; and in that event subsection (4) shall not apply, but the notice shall not require the information to be furnished before the end of the period of seven days beginning with the day on which the notice is served.

(6) A person shall not be required by virtue of this section to furnish the Commissioner with any information in respect of—

(a) any communication between a professional legal adviser and his client in connection with the giving of legal advice to the client with respect to his obligations, liabilities or rights under this Act, or

(b) any communication between a professional legal adviser and his client, or between such an adviser or his client and any other person, made in connection with or in contemplation of proceedings under or arising out of this Act (including proceedings before the Tribunal) and for the purposes of such proceedings.

(7) In subsection (6) references to the client of a professional legal adviser include references to any person representing such a client.

(8) A person shall not be required by virtue of this section to furnish the Commissioner with any information if the furnishing of that information would, by revealing evidence of the commission of any offence other than an offence under this Act, expose him to proceedings for that offence.

(9) The Commissioner may cancel an information notice by written notice to the person on whom it was served.

(10) This section has effect subject to section 46(3).

44 Special information notices

(1) If the Commissioner—

(a) has received a request under section 42 in respect of any processing of personal data, or

(b) has reasonable grounds for suspecting that, in a case in which proceedings have been stayed under section 32, the personal data to which the proceedings relate—

(i) are not being processed only for the special purposes, or

(ii) are not being processed with a view to the publication by any person of any journalistic, literary or artistic material which has not previously been published by the data controller,

he may serve the data controller with a notice (in this Act referred to as a "special information notice") requiring the data controller, within such time as is specified in the notice, to furnish the Commissioner, in such form as may be so specified, with such information as is so specified for the purpose specified in subsection (2).

(2) That purpose is the purpose of ascertaining—

(a) whether the personal data are being processed only for the special purposes, or

(b) whether they are being processed with a view to the publication by any person of any journalistic, literary or artistic material which has not previously been published by the data controller.

(3) A special information notice must contain—

(a) in a case falling within paragraph (a) of subsection (1), a statement that the Commissioner has received a request under section 42 in relation to the specified processing, or

(b) in a case falling within paragraph (b) of that subsection, a statement of the Commissioner's grounds for suspecting that the personal data are not being processed as mentioned in that paragraph.

(4) A special information notice must also contain particulars of the rights of appeal conferred by section 48.

(5) Subject to subsection (6), the time specified in a special information notice shall not expire before the end of the period within which an appeal can be brought against the notice and, if such an appeal is brought, the information need not be furnished pending the determination or withdrawal of the appeal.

(6) If by reason of special circumstances the Commissioner considers that the information is required as a matter of urgency, he may include in the notice a statement to that effect and a statement of his reasons for reaching that conclusion; and in that event subsection (5) shall not apply, but the notice shall not require the information to be furnished before the end of the period of seven days beginning with the day on which the notice is served.

(7) A person shall not be required by virtue of this section to furnish the Commissioner with any information in respect of—

(a) any communication between a professional legal adviser and his client in connection with the giving of legal advice to the client with respect to his obligations, liabilities or rights under this Act, or

(b) any communication between a professional legal adviser and his client, or between such an adviser or his client and any other person, made in connection with or in contemplation of proceedings under or arising out of this Act (including proceedings before the Tribunal) and for the purposes of such proceedings.

(8) In subsection (7) references to the client of a professional legal adviser include references to any person representing such a client.

(9) A person shall not be required by virtue of this section to furnish the Commissioner with any information if the furnishing of that information would, by revealing evidence of the commission of any offence other than an offence under this Act, expose him to proceedings for that offence.

(10) The Commissioner may cancel a special information notice by written notice to the person on whom it was served.

45 Determination by Commissioner as to the special purposes

(1) Where at any time it appears to the Commissioner (whether as a result of the service of a special information notice or otherwise) that any personal data—

(a) are not being processed only for the special purposes, or

(b) are not being processed with a view to the publication by any person of any journalistic, literary or artistic material which has not previously been published by the data controller,

he may make a determination in writing to that effect.

(2) Notice of the determination shall be given to the data controller; and the notice must contain particulars of the right of appeal conferred by section 48.

(3) A determination under subsection (1) shall not take effect until the end of the period within which an appeal can be brought and, where an appeal is brought, shall not take effect pending the determination or withdrawal of the appeal.

46 Restriction on enforcement in case of processing for the special purposes

(1) The Commissioner may not at any time serve an enforcement notice on a data controller with respect to the processing of personal data for the special purposes unless—

(a) a determination under section 45(1) with respect to those data has taken effect, and

(b) the court has granted leave for the notice to be served.

(2) The court shall not grant leave for the purposes of subsection (1)(b) unless it is satisfied—

(a) that the Commissioner has reason to suspect a contravention of the data protection principles which is of substantial public importance, and

(b) except where the case is one of urgency, that the data controller has been given notice, in accordance with rules of court, of the application for leave.

(3) The Commissioner may not serve an information notice on a data controller with respect to the processing of personal data for the special purposes unless a determination under section 45(1) with respect to those data has taken effect.

47 Failure to comply with notice

(1) A person who fails to comply with an enforcement notice, an information notice or a special information notice is guilty of an offence.

(2) A person who, in purported compliance with an information notice or a special information notice—

(a) makes a statement which he knows to be false in a material respect, or

(b) recklessly makes a statement which is false in a material respect,

is guilty of an offence.

(3) It is a defence for a person charged with an offence under subsection (1) to prove that he exercised all due diligence to comply with the notice in question.

48 Rights of appeal

(1) A person on whom an enforcement notice, an information notice or a special information notice has been served may appeal to the Tribunal against the notice.

(2) A person on whom an enforcement notice has been served may appeal to the Tribunal against the refusal of an application under section 41(2) for cancellation or variation of the notice.

(3) Where an enforcement notice, an information notice or a special information notice contains a statement by the Commissioner in accordance with section 40(8), 43(5) or 44(6) then, whether or not the person appeals against the notice, he may appeal against—

(a) the Commissioner's decision to include the statement in the notice, or

(b) the effect of the inclusion of the statement as respects any part of the notice.

(4) A data controller in respect of whom a determination has been made under section 45 may appeal to the Tribunal against the determination.

(5) Schedule 6 has effect in relation to appeals under this section and the proceedings of the Tribunal in respect of any such appeal.

49 Determination of appeals

(1) If on an appeal under section 48(1) the Tribunal considers—

(a) that the notice against which the appeal is brought is not in accordance with the law, or

(b) to the extent that the notice involved an exercise of discretion by the Commissioner, that he ought to have exercised his discretion differently,

the Tribunal shall allow the appeal or substitute such other notice or decision as could have been served or made by the Commissioner; and in any other case the Tribunal shall dismiss the appeal.

(2) On such an appeal, the Tribunal may review any determination of fact on which the notice in question was based.

(3) If on an appeal under section 48(2) the Tribunal considers that the enforcement notice ought to be cancelled or varied by reason of a change in circumstances, the Tribunal shall cancel or vary the notice.

(4) On an appeal under subsection (3) of section 48 the Tribunal may direct—

(a) that the notice in question shall have effect as if it did not contain any such statement as is mentioned in that subsection, or

(b) that the inclusion of the statement shall not have effect in relation to any part of the notice,

and may make such modifications in the notice as may be required for giving effect to the direction.

(5) On an appeal under section 48(4), the Tribunal may cancel the determination of the Commissioner.

(6) Any party to an appeal to the Tribunal under section 48 may appeal from the decision of the Tribunal on a point of law to the appropriate court; and that court shall be—

(a) the High Court of Justice in England if the address of the person who was the appellant before the Tribunal is in England or Wales,

(b) the Court of Session if that address is in Scotland, and

(c) the High Court of Justice in Northern Ireland if that address is in Northern Ireland.

(7) For the purposes of subsection (6)—

(a) the address of a registered company is that of its registered office, and

(b) the address of a person (other than a registered company) carrying on a business is that of his principal place of business in the United Kingdom.

50 Powers of entry and inspection

Schedule 9 (powers of entry and inspection) has effect.

PART VI

MISCELLANEOUS AND GENERAL

Functions of Commissioner

51 General duties of Commissioner

(1) It shall be the duty of the Commissioner to promote the following of good practice by data controllers and, in particular, so to perform his functions under this Act as to promote the observance of the requirements of this Act by data controllers.

(2) The Commissioner shall arrange for the dissemination in such form and manner as he considers appropriate of such information as it may appear to him expedient to give to the public about the operation of this Act, about good practice, and about other matters within the scope of his functions under this Act, and may give advice to any person as to any of those matters.

(3) Where—

(a) the Secretary of State so directs by order, or

(b) the Commissioner considers it appropriate to do so,

the Commissioner shall, after such consultation with trade associations, data subjects or persons representing data subjects as appears to him to be appropriate, prepare and disseminate to such persons as he considers appropriate codes of practice for guidance as to good practice.

(4) The Commissioner shall also—

(a) where he considers it appropriate to do so, encourage trade associations to prepare, and to disseminate to their members, such codes of practice, and

(b) where any trade association submits a code of practice to him for his consideration, consider the code and, after such consultation with data subjects or persons representing data subjects as appears to him to be appropriate, notify the trade association whether in his opinion the code promotes the following of good practice.

(5) An order under subsection (3) shall describe the personal data or processing to which the code of practice is to relate, and may also describe the persons or classes of persons to whom it is to relate.

(6) The Commissioner shall arrange for the dissemination in such form and manner as he considers appropriate of—

(a) any Community finding as defined by paragraph 15(2) of Part II of Schedule 1,

(b) any decision of the European Commission, under the procedure provided for in Article 31(2) of the Data Protection Directive, which is made for the purposes of Article 26(3) or (4) of the Directive, and

(c) such other information as it may appear to him to be expedient to give to data controllers in relation to any personal data about the protection of the rights and freedoms of data subjects in relation to the processing of personal data in countries and territories outside the European Economic Area.

(7) The Commissioner may, with the consent of the data controller, assess any processing of personal data for the following of good practice and shall inform the data controller of the results of the assessment.

(8) The Commissioner may charge such sums as he may with the consent of the Secretary of State determine for any services provided by the Commissioner by virtue of this Part.

(9) In this section—

"good practice" means such practice in the processing of personal data as appears to the Commissioner to be desirable having regard to the interests of data subjects and others, and includes (but is not limited to) compliance with the requirements of this Act;

"trade association" includes any body representing data controllers.

52 Reports and codes of practice to be laid before Parliament

(1) The Commissioner shall lay annually before each House of Parliament a general report on the exercise of his functions under this Act.

(2) The Commissioner may from time to time lay before each House of Parliament such other reports with respect to those functions as he thinks fit.

(3) The Commissioner shall lay before each House of Parliament any code of practice prepared under section 51(3) for complying with a direction of the Secretary of State, unless the code is included in any report laid under subsection (1) or (2).

53 Assistance by Commissioner in cases involving processing for the special purposes

(1) An individual who is an actual or prospective party to any proceedings under section 7(9), 10(4), 12(8) or 14 or by virtue of section 13 which relate to personal data processed for the special purposes may apply to the Commissioner for assistance in relation to those proceedings.

(2) The Commissioner shall, as soon as reasonably practicable after receiving an application under subsection (1), consider it and decide whether and to what extent to grant it, but he shall not grant the application unless, in his opinion, the case involves a matter of substantial public importance.

(3) If the Commissioner decides to provide assistance, he shall, as soon as reasonably practicable after making the decision, notify the applicant, stating the extent of the assistance to be provided.

(4) If the Commissioner decides not to provide assistance, he shall, as soon as reasonably practicable after making the decision, notify the applicant of his decision and, if he thinks fit, the reasons for it.

(5) In this section—

(a) references to "proceedings" include references to prospective proceedings, and

(b) "applicant", in relation to assistance under this section, means an individual who applies for assistance.

(6) Schedule 10 has effect for supplementing this section.

54 International co-operation

(1) The Commissioner—

(a) shall continue to be the designated authority in the United Kingdom for the purposes of Article 13 of the Convention, and

(b) shall be the supervisory authority in the United Kingdom for the purposes of the Data Protection Directive.

(2) The Secretary of State may by order make provision as to the functions to be discharged by the Commissioner as the designated authority in the United Kingdom for the purposes of Article 13 of the Convention.

(3) The Secretary of State may by order make provision as to co-operation by the Commissioner with the European Commission and with supervisory authorities in other EEA States in connection with the performance of their respective duties and, in particular, as to—

(a) the exchange of information with supervisory authorities in other EEA States or with the European Commission, and

(b) the exercise within the United Kingdom at the request of a supervisory authority in another EEA State, in cases excluded by section 5 from the application of the other provisions of this Act, of functions of the Commissioner specified in the order.

(4) The Commissioner shall also carry out any data protection functions which the Secretary of State may by order direct him to carry out for the purpose of enabling Her Majesty's Government in the United Kingdom to give effect to any international obligations of the United Kingdom.

(5) The Commissioner shall, if so directed by the Secretary of State, provide any authority exercising data protection functions under the law of a colony specified in the direction with such assistance in connection with the discharge of those functions as the Secretary of State may direct or approve, on such terms (including terms as to payment) as the Secretary of State may direct or approve.

(6) Where the European Commission makes a decision for the purposes of Article 26(3) or (4) of the Data Protection Directive under the procedure provided for in Article 31(2) of the Directive, the Commissioner shall comply with that decision in exercising his functions under paragraph 9 of Schedule 4 or, as the case may be, paragraph 8 of that Schedule.

(7) The Commissioner shall inform the European Commission and the supervisory authorities in other EEA States—

(a) of any approvals granted for the purposes of paragraph 8 of Schedule 4, and

(b) of any authorisations granted for the purposes of paragraph 9 of that Schedule.

(8) In this section—

"the Convention" means the Convention for the Protection of Individuals with regard to Automatic Processing of Personal Data which was opened for signature on 28th January 1981;

"data protection functions" means functions relating to the protection of individuals with respect to the processing of personal information.

Unlawful obtaining etc. of personal data

55 Unlawful obtaining etc. of personal data

(1) A person must not knowingly or recklessly, without the consent of the data controller—

(a) obtain or disclose personal data or the information contained in personal data, or

(b) procure the disclosure to another person of the information contained in personal data.

(2) Subsection (1) does not apply to a person who shows—

(a) that the obtaining, disclosing or procuring—

(i) was necessary for the purpose of preventing or detecting crime, or

(ii) was required or authorised by or under any enactment, by any rule of law or by the order of a court,

(b) that he acted in the reasonable belief that he had in law the right to obtain or disclose the data or information or, as the case may be, to procure the disclosure of the information to the other person,

(c) that he acted in the reasonable belief that he would have had the consent of the data controller if the data controller had known of the obtaining, disclosing or procuring and the circumstances of it, or

(d) that in the particular circumstances the obtaining, disclosing or procuring was justified as being in the public interest.

(3) A person who contravenes subsection (1) is guilty of an offence.

(4) A person who sells personal data is guilty of an offence if he has obtained the data in contravention of subsection (1).

(5) A person who offers to sell personal data is guilty of an offence if—

(a) he has obtained the data in contravention of subsection (1), or

(b) he subsequently obtains the data in contravention of that subsection.

(6) For the purposes of subsection (5), an advertisement indicating that personal data are or may be for sale is an offer to sell the data.

(7) Section 1(2) does not apply for the purposes of this section; and for the purposes of subsections (4) to (6), "personal data" includes information extracted from personal data.

(8) References in this section to personal data do not include references to personal data which by virtue of section 28 are exempt from this section.

Records obtained under data subject's right of access

56 Prohibition of requirement as to production of certain records

(1) A person must not, in connection with—

(a) the recruitment of another person as an employee,

(b) the continued employment of another person, or

(c) any contract for the provision of services to him by another person, require that other person or a third party to supply him with a relevant record or to produce a relevant record to him.

(2) A person concerned with the provision (for payment or not) of goods, facilities or services to the public or a section of the public must not, as a condition of providing or offering to provide any goods, facilities or services to another person, require that other person or a third party to supply him with a relevant record or to produce a relevant record to him.

(3) Subsections (1) and (2) do not apply to a person who shows—

(a) that the imposition of the requirement was required or authorised by or under any enactment, by any rule of law or by the order of a court, or

(b) that in the particular circumstances the imposition of the requirement was justified as being in the public interest.

(4) Having regard to the provisions of Part V of the Police Act 1997 (certificates of criminal records etc.), the imposition of the requirement referred to in subsection (1) or (2) is not to be regarded as being justified as being in the public interest on the ground that it would assist in the prevention or detection of crime.

(5) A person who contravenes subsection (1) or (2) is guilty of an offence.

(6) In this section "a relevant record" means any record which—

(a) has been or is to be obtained by a data subject from any data controller specified in the first column of the Table below in the exercise of the right conferred by section 7, and

(b) contains information relating to any matter specified in relation to that data controller in the second column,

and includes a copy of such a record or a part of such a record.

TABLE

Data controller	*Subject-matter*
1. Any of the following persons— (a) a chief officer of police of a police force in England and Wales. (b) a chief constable of a police force in Scotland. (c) the Chief Constable of the Royal Ulster Constabulary. (d) the Director General of the National Criminal Intelligence Service. (e) the Director General of the National Crime Squad.	(a) Convictions. (b) Cautions.
2. The Secretary of State.	(a) Convictions. (b) Cautions. (c) His functions under section 53 of the Children and Young Persons Act 1933, section 205(2) or 208 of the Criminal Procedure (Scotland) Act 1995 or section 73 of the

Data controller	*Subject-matter*
	Children and Young Persons Act (Northern Ireland) 1968 in relation to any person sentenced to detention. (d) His functions under the Prison Act 1952, the Prisons (Scotland) Act 1989 or the Prison Act (Northern Ireland) 1953 in relation to any person imprisoned or detained. (e) His functions under the Social Security Contributions and Benefits Act 1992, the Social Security Administration Act 1992 or the Jobseekers Act 1995. (f) His functions under Part V of the Police Act 1997.
3. The Department of Health and Social Services for Northern Ireland.	Its functions under the Social Security Contributions and Benefits (Northern Ireland) Act 1992, the Social Security Administration (Northern Ireland) Act 1992 or the Jobseekers (Northern Ireland) Order 1995.

(7) In the Table in subsection (6)—

"caution" means a caution given to any person in England and Wales or Northern Ireland in respect of an offence which, at the time when the caution is given, is admitted;

"conviction" has the same meaning as in the Rehabilitation of Offenders Act 1974 or the Rehabilitation of Offenders (Northern Ireland) Order 1978.

(8) The Secretary of State may by order amend—

(a) the Table in subsection (6), and

(b) subsection (7).

(9) For the purposes of this section a record which states that a data controller is not processing any personal data relating to a particular matter shall be taken to be a record containing information relating to that matter.

(10) In this section "employee" means an individual who—

(a) works under a contract of employment, as defined by section 230(2) of the Employment Rights Act 1996, or

(b) holds any office,

whether or not he is entitled to remuneration; and "employment" shall be construed accordingly.

57 Avoidance of certain contractual terms relating to health records

(1) Any term or condition of a contract is void in so far as it purports to require an individual—

(a) to supply any other person with a record to which this section applies, or with a copy of such a record or a part of such a record, or

(b) to produce to any other person such a record, copy or part.

(2) This section applies to any record which—

(a) has been or is to be obtained by a data subject in the exercise of the right conferred by section 7, and

(b) consists of the information contained in any health record as defined by section 68(2).

Information provided to Commissioner or Tribunal

58 Disclosure of information

No enactment or rule of law prohibiting or restricting the disclosure of information shall preclude a person from furnishing the Commissioner or the Tribunal with any information necessary for the discharge of their functions under this Act.

59 Confidentiality of information

(1) No person who is or has been the Commissioner, a member of the Commissioner's staff or an agent of the Commissioner shall disclose any information which—

(a) has been obtained by, or furnished to, the Commissioner under or for the purposes of this Act,

(b) relates to an identified or identifiable individual or business, and

(c) is not at the time of the disclosure, and has not previously been, available to the public from other sources,

unless the disclosure is made with lawful authority.

(2) For the purposes of subsection (1) a disclosure of information is made with lawful authority only if, and to the extent that—

(a) the disclosure is made with the consent of the individual or of the person for the time being carrying on the business,

(b) the information was provided for the purpose of its being made available to the public (in whatever manner) under any provision of this Act,

(c) the disclosure is made for the purposes of, and is necessary for, the discharge of—

(i) any functions under this Act, or

(ii) any Community obligation,

(d) the disclosure is made for the purposes of any proceedings, whether criminal or civil and whether arising under, or by virtue of, this Act or otherwise, or

(e) having regard to the rights and freedoms or legitimate interests of any person, the disclosure is necessary in the public interest.

(3) Any person who knowingly or recklessly discloses information in contravention of subsection (1) is guilty of an offence.

General provisions relating to offences

60 Prosecutions and penalties

(1) No proceedings for an offence under this Act shall be instituted—

(a) in England or Wales, except by the Commissioner or by or with the consent of the Director of Public Prosecutions;

(b) in Northern Ireland, except by the Commissioner or by or with the consent of the Director of Public Prosecutions for Northern Ireland.

(2) A person guilty of an offence under any provision of this Act other than paragraph 12 of Schedule 9 is liable—

(a) on summary conviction, to a fine not exceeding the statutory maximum, or

(b) on conviction on indictment, to a fine.

(3) A person guilty of an offence under paragraph 12 of Schedule 9 is liable on summary conviction to a fine not exceeding level 5 on the standard scale.

(4) Subject to subsection (5), the court by or before which a person is convicted of—

(a) an offence under section 21(1), 22(6), 55 or 56,

(b) an offence under section 21(2) relating to processing which is assessable processing for the purposes of section 22, or

(c) an offence under section 47(1) relating to an enforcement notice,

may order any document or other material used in connection with the processing of personal data and appearing to the court to be connected with the commission of the offence to be forfeited, destroyed or erased.

(5) The court shall not make an order under subsection (4) in relation to any material where a person (other than the offender) claiming to be the owner of or otherwise interested in the material applies to be heard by the court, unless an opportunity is given to him to show cause why the order should not be made.

61 Liability of directors etc

(1) Where an offence under this Act has been committed by a body corporate and is proved to have been committed with the consent or connivance of or to be attributable to any neglect on the part of any director, manager, secretary or similar officer of the body corporate or any person who was purporting to act in any such capacity, he as well as the body corporate shall be guilty of that offence and be liable to be proceeded against and punished accordingly.

(2) Where the affairs of a body corporate are managed by its members subsection (1) shall apply in relation to the acts and defaults of a member in connection with his functions of management as if he were a director of the body corporate.

(3) Where an offence under this Act has been committed by a Scottish partnership and the contravention in question is proved to have occurred with the consent or connivance of, or to be attributable to any neglect on the part of, a partner, he as well as the partnership shall be guilty of that offence and shall be liable to be proceeded against and punished accordingly.

Amendments of Consumer Credit Act 1974

62 Amendments of Consumer Credit Act 1974

(1) In section 158 of the Consumer Credit Act 1974 (duty of agency to disclose filed information)—

(a) in subsection (1)—

(i) in paragraph (a) for "individual" there is substituted "partnership or other unincorporated body of persons not consisting entirely of bodies corporate", and

(ii) for "him" there is substituted "it",

(b) in subsection (2), for "his" there is substituted "the consumer's", and

(c) in subsection (3), for "him" there is substituted "the consumer".

(2) In section 159 of that Act (correction of wrong information) for subsection (1) there is substituted—

"(1) Any individual (the "objector") given—

(a) information under section 7 of the Data Protection Act 1998 by a credit reference agency, or

(b) information under section 158,

who considers that an entry in his file is incorrect, and that if it is not corrected he is likely to be prejudiced, may give notice to the agency requiring it either to remove the entry from the file or amend it."

(3) In subsections (2) to (6) of that section—

(a) for "consumer", wherever occurring, there is substituted "objector", and

(b) for "Director", wherever occurring, there is substituted "the relevant authority".

(4) After subsection (6) of that section there is inserted—

"(7) The Data Protection Commissioner may vary or revoke any order made by him under this section.

(8) In this section "the relevant authority" means—

(a) where the objector is a partnership or other unincorporated body of persons, the Director, and

(b) in any other case, the Data Protection Commissioner."

(5) In section 160 of that Act (alternative procedure for business consumers)—

(a) in subsection (4)—

(i) for "him" there is substituted "to the consumer", and

(ii) in paragraphs (a) and (b) for "he" there is substituted "the consumer" and for "his" there is substituted "the consumer's", and

(b) after subsection (6) there is inserted—

"(7) In this section "consumer" has the same meaning as in section 158."

General

63 Application to Crown

(1) This Act binds the Crown.

(2) For the purposes of this Act each government department shall be treated as a person separate from any other government department.

(3) Where the purposes for which and the manner in which any personal data are, or are to be, processed are determined by any person acting on behalf of the Royal Household, the Duchy of Lancaster or the Duchy of Cornwall, the data controller in respect of those data for the purposes of this Act shall be—

(a) in relation to the Royal Household, the Keeper of the Privy Purse,

(b) in relation to the Duchy of Lancaster, such person as the Chancellor of the Duchy appoints, and

(c) in relation to the Duchy of Cornwall, such person as the Duke of Cornwall, or the possessor for the time being of the Duchy of Cornwall, appoints.

(4) Different persons may be appointed under subsection (3)(b) or (c) for different purposes.

(5) Neither a government department nor a person who is a data controller by virtue of subsection (3) shall be liable to prosecution under this Act, but section 55 and paragraph 12 of Schedule 9 shall apply to a person in the service of the Crown as they apply to any other person.

64 Transmission of notices etc. by electronic or other means

(1) This section applies to—

(a) a notice or request under any provision of Part II,

(b) a notice under subsection (1) of section 24 or particulars made available under that subsection, or

(c) an application under section 41(2),

but does not apply to anything which is required to be served in accordance with rules of court.

(2) The requirement that any notice, request, particulars or application to which this section applies should be in writing is satisfied where the text of the notice, request, particulars or application—

(a) is transmitted by electronic means,

(b) is received in legible form, and

(c) is capable of being used for subsequent reference.

(3) The Secretary of State may by regulations provide that any requirement that any notice, request, particulars or application to which this section applies should be in writing is not to apply in such circumstances as may be prescribed by the regulations.

65 Service of notices by Commissioner

(1) Any notice authorised or required by this Act to be served on or given to any person by the Commissioner may—

(a) if that person is an individual, be served on him—
   (i) by delivering it to him, or
   (ii) by sending it to him by post addressed to him at his usual or last-known place of residence or business, or
   (iii) by leaving it for him at that place;
(b) if that person is a body corporate or unincorporate, be served on that body—
   (i) by sending it by post to the proper officer of the body at its principal office, or
   (ii) by addressing it to the proper officer of the body and leaving it at that office;
(c) if that person is a partnership in Scotland, be served on that partnership—
   (i) by sending it by post to the principal office of the partnership, or
   (ii) by addressing it to that partnership and leaving it at that office.

(2) In subsection (1)(b) "principal office", in relation to a registered company, means its registered office and "proper officer", in relation to any body, means the secretary or other executive officer charged with the conduct of its general affairs.

(3) This section is without prejudice to any other lawful method of serving or giving a notice.

66 Exercise of rights in Scotland by children

(1) Where a question falls to be determined in Scotland as to the legal capacity of a person under the age of sixteen years to exercise any right conferred by any provision of this Act, that person shall be taken to have that capacity where he has a general understanding of what it means to exercise that right.

(2) Without prejudice to the generality of subsection (1), a person of twelve years of age or more shall be presumed to be of sufficient age and maturity to have such understanding as is mentioned in that subsection.

67 Orders, regulations and rules

(1) Any power conferred by this Act on the Secretary of State to make an order, regulations or rules shall be exercisable by statutory instrument.

(2) Any order, regulations or rules made by the Secretary of State under this Act may—
(a) make different provision for different cases, and
(b) make such supplemental, incidental, consequential or transitional provision or savings as the Secretary of State considers appropriate;

and nothing in section 7(11), 19(5), 26(1) or 30(4) limits the generality of paragraph (a).

(3) Before making—
(a) an order under any provision of this Act other than section 75(3),
(b) any regulations under this Act other than notification regulations (as defined by section 16(2)),

the Secretary of State shall consult the Commissioner.

(4) A statutory instrument containing (whether alone or with other provisions) an order under—

section 10(2)(b),
section 12(5)(b),
section 22(1),
section 30,
section 32(3),
section 38,
section 56(8),
paragraph 10 of Schedule 3, or
paragraph 4 of Schedule 7,

shall not be made unless a draft of the instrument has been laid before and approved by a resolution of each House of Parliament.

(5) A statutory instrument which contains (whether alone or with other provisions)—

(a) an order under—

section 22(7),
section 23,
section 51(3),
section 54(2), (3) or (4),
paragraph 3, 4 or 14 of Part II of Schedule 1,
paragraph 6 of Schedule 2,
paragraph 2, 7 or 9 of Schedule 3,
paragraph 4 of Schedule 4,
paragraph 6 of Schedule 7,

(b) regulations under section 7 which—

(i) prescribe cases for the purposes of subsection (2)(b),

(ii) are made by virtue of subsection (7), or

(iii) relate to the definition of "the prescribed period",

(c) regulations under section 8(1) or 9(3),

(d) regulations under section 64,

(e) notification regulations (as defined by section 16(2)), or

(f) rules under paragraph 7 of Schedule 6,

and which is not subject to the requirement in subsection (4) that a draft of the instrument be laid before and approved by a resolution of each House of Parliament, shall be subject to annulment in pursuance of a resolution of either House of Parliament.

(6) A statutory instrument which contains only—

(a) regulations prescribing fees for the purposes of any provision of this Act, or

(b) regulations under section 7 prescribing fees for the purposes of any other enactment,

shall be laid before Parliament after being made.

68 Meaning of "accessible record"

(1) In this Act "accessible record" means—

(a) a health record as defined by subsection (2),

(b) an educational record as defined by Schedule 11, or

(c) an accessible public record as defined by Schedule 12.

(2) In subsection (1)(a) "health record" means any record which—
(a) consists of information relating to the physical or mental health or condition of an individual, and
(b) has been made by or on behalf of a health professional in connection with the care of that individual.

69 Meaning of "health professional"

(1) In this Act "health professional" means any of the following—
(a) a registered medical practitioner,
(b) a registered dentist as defined by section 53(1) of the Dentists Act 1984,
(c) a registered optician as defined by section 36(1) of the Opticians Act 1989,
(d) a registered pharmaceutical chemist as defined by section 24(1) of the Pharmacy Act 1954 or a registered person as defined by Article 2(2) of the Pharmacy (Northern Ireland) Order 1976,
(e) a registered nurse, midwife or health visitor,
(f) a registered osteopath as defined by section 41 of the Osteopaths Act 1993,
(g) a registered chiropractor as defined by section 43 of the Chiropractors Act 1994,
(h) any person who is registered as a member of a profession to which the Professions Supplementary to Medicine Act 1960 for the time being extends,
(i) a clinical psychologist, child psychotherapist or speech therapist,
(j) a music therapist employed by a health service body, and
(k) a scientist employed by such a body as head of a department.

(2) In subsection (1)(a) "registered medical practitioner" includes any person who is provisionally registered under section 15 or 21 of the Medical Act 1983 and is engaged in such employment as is mentioned in subsection (3) of that section.

(3) In subsection (1) "health service body" means—
(a) a Health Authority established under section 8 of the National Health Service Act 1977,
(b) a Special Health Authority established under section 11 of that Act,
(c) a Health Board within the meaning of the National Health Service (Scotland) Act 1978,
(d) a Special Health Board within the meaning of that Act,
(e) the managers of a State Hospital provided under section 102 of that Act,
(f) a National Health Service trust first established under section 5 of the National Health Service and Community Care Act 1990 or section 12A of the National Health Service (Scotland) Act 1978,
(g) a Health and Social Services Board established under Article 16 of the Health and Personal Social Services (Northern Ireland) Order 1972,
(h) a special health and social services agency established under the Health and Personal Social Services (Special Agencies) (Northern Ireland) Order 1990, or
(i) a Health and Social Services trust established under Article 10 of the Health and Personal Social Services (Northern Ireland) Order 1991.

70 Supplementary definitions

(1) In this Act, unless the context otherwise requires—

"business" includes any trade or profession;

"the Commissioner" means the Data Protection Commissioner;

"credit reference agency" has the same meaning as in the Consumer Credit Act 1974;

"the Data Protection Directive" means Directive 95/46/EC on the protection of individuals with regard to the processing of personal data and on the free movement of such data;

"EEA State" means a State which is a contracting party to the Agreement on the European Economic Area signed at Oporto on 2nd May 1992 as adjusted by the Protocol signed at Brussels on 17th March 1993;

"enactment" includes an enactment passed after this Act;

"government department" includes a Northern Ireland department and any body or authority exercising statutory functions on behalf of the Crown;

"Minister of the Crown" has the same meaning as in the Ministers of the Crown Act 1975;

"public register" means any register which pursuant to a requirement imposed—

(a) by or under any enactment, or

(b) in pursuance of any international agreement,

is open to public inspection or open to inspection by any person having a legitimate interest;

"pupil"—

(a) in relation to a school in England and Wales, means a registered pupil within the meaning of the Education Act 1996,

(b) in relation to a school in Scotland, means a pupil within the meaning of the Education (Scotland) Act 1980, and

(c) in relation to a school in Northern Ireland, means a registered pupil within the meaning of the Education and Libraries (Northern Ireland) Order 1986;

"recipient", in relation to any personal data, means any person to whom the data are disclosed, including any person (such as an employee or agent of the data controller, a data processor or an employee or agent of a data processor) to whom they are disclosed in the course of processing the data for the data controller, but does not include any person to whom disclosure is or may be made as a result of, or with a view to, a particular inquiry by or on behalf of that person made in the exercise of any power conferred by law;

"registered company" means a company registered under the enactments relating to companies for the time being in force in the United Kingdom;

"school"—

(a) in relation to England and Wales, has the same meaning as in the Education Act 1996,

(b) in relation to Scotland, has the same meaning as in the Education (Scotland) Act 1980, and

(c) in relation to Northern Ireland, has the same meaning as in the Education and Libraries (Northern Ireland) Order 1986;

"teacher" includes—

(a) in Great Britain, head teacher, and
(b) in Northern Ireland, the principal of a school;

"third party", in relation to personal data, means any person other than—

(a) the data subject,
(b) the data controller, or
(c) any data processor or other person authorised to process data for the data controller or processor;

"the Tribunal" means the Data Protection Tribunal.

(2) For the purposes of this Act data are inaccurate if they are incorrect or misleading as to any matter of fact.

71 Index of defined expressions

The following Table shows provisions defining or otherwise explaining expressions used in this Act (other than provisions defining or explaining an expression only used in the same section or Schedule)—

accessible record	section 68
address (in Part III)	section 16(3)
business	section 70(1)
the Commissioner	section 70(1)
credit reference agency	section 70(1)
data	section 1(1)
data controller	sections 1(1) and (4) and 63(3)
data processor	section 1(1)
the Data Protection Directive	section 70(1)
data protection principles	section 4 and Schedule 1
data subject	section 1(1)
disclosing (of personal data)	section 1(2)(b)
EEA State	section 70(1)
enactment	section 70(1)
enforcement notice	section 40(1)
fees regulations (in Part III)	section 16(2)
government department	section 70(1)
health professional	section 69
inaccurate (in relation to data)	section 70(2)
information notice	section 43(1)
Minister of the Crown	section 70(1)
the non-disclosure provisions (in Part IV)	section 27(3)

notification regulations (in Part III)	section 16(2)
obtaining (of personal data)	section 1(2)(a)
personal data	section 1(1)
prescribed (in Part III)	section 16(2)
processing (of information or data)	section 1(1) and paragraph 5 of Schedule 8
public register	section 70(1)
publish (in relation to journalistic, literary or artistic material)	section 32(6)
pupil (in relation to a school)	section 70(1)
recipient (in relation to personal data)	section 70(1)
recording (of personal data)	section 1(2)(a)
registered company	section 70(1)
registrable particulars (in Part III)	section 16(1)
relevant filing system	section 1(1)
school	section 70(1)
sensitive personal data	section 2
special information notice	section 44(1)
the special purposes	section 3
the subject information provisions (in Part IV)	section 27(2)
teacher	section 70(1)
third party (in relation to processing of personal data)	section 70(1)
the Tribunal	section 70(1)
using (of personal data)	section 1(2)(b).

72 Modifications of Act

During the period beginning with the commencement of this section and ending with 23rd October 2007, the provisions of this Act shall have effect subject to the modifications set out in Schedule 13.

73 Transitional provisions and savings

Schedule 14 (which contains transitional provisions and savings) has effect.

74 Minor and consequential amendments and repeals and revocations

(1) Schedule 15 (which contains minor and consequential amendments) has effect.

(2) The enactments and instruments specified in Schedule 16 are repealed or revoked to the extent specified.

75 Short title, commencement and extent

(1) This Act may be cited as the Data Protection Act 1998.

(2) The following provisions of this Act—

(a) sections 1 to 3,

(b) section 25(1) and (4),

(c) section 26,

(d) sections 67 to 71,

(e) this section,

(f) paragraph 17 of Schedule 5,

(g) Schedule 11,

(h) Schedule 12, and

(i) so much of any other provision of this Act as confers any power to make subordinate legislation,

shall come into force on the day on which this Act is passed.

(3) The remaining provisions of this Act shall come into force on such day as the Secretary of State may by order appoint; and different days may be appointed for different purposes.

(4) The day appointed under subsection (3) for the coming into force of section 56 must not be earlier than the first day on which sections 112, 113 and 115 of the Police Act 1997 (which provide for the issue by the Secretary of State of criminal conviction certificates, criminal record certificates and enhanced criminal record certificates) are all in force.

(5) Subject to subsection (6), this Act extends to Northern Ireland.

(6) Any amendment, repeal or revocation made by Schedule 15 or 16 has the same extent as that of the enactment or instrument to which it relates.

SCHEDULES

SCHEDULE 1

Section 4(1) and (2).

THE DATA PROTECTION PRINCIPLES

PART I

THE PRINCIPLES

1 Personal data shall be processed fairly and lawfully and, in particular, shall not be processed unless—

(a) at least one of the conditions in Schedule 2 is met, and

(b) in the case of sensitive personal data, at least one of the conditions in Schedule 3 is also met.

2 Personal data shall be obtained only for one or more specified and lawful purposes, and shall not be further processed in any manner incompatible with that purpose or those purposes.

3 Personal data shall be adequate, relevant and not excessive in relation to the purpose or purposes for which they are processed.

4 Personal data shall be accurate and, where necessary, kept up to date.

5 Personal data processed for any purpose or purposes shall not be kept for longer than is necessary for that purpose or those purposes.

6 Personal data shall be processed in accordance with the rights of data subjects under this Act.

7 Appropriate technical and organisational measures shall be taken against unauthorised or unlawful processing of personal data and against accidental loss or destruction of, or damage to, personal data.

8 Personal data shall not be transferred to a country or territory outside the European Economic Area unless that country or territory ensures an adequate level of protection for the rights and freedoms of data subjects in relation to the processing of personal data.

PART II

INTERPRETATION OF THE PRINCIPLES IN PART I

The first principle

1 (1) In determining for the purposes of the first principle whether personal data are processed fairly, regard is to be had to the method by which they are obtained,

including in particular whether any person from whom they are obtained is deceived or misled as to the purpose or purposes for which they are to be processed.

(2) Subject to paragraph 2, for the purposes of the first principle data are to be treated as obtained fairly if they consist of information obtained from a person who—

(a) is authorised by or under any enactment to supply it, or

(b) is required to supply it by or under any enactment or by any convention or other instrument imposing an international obligation on the United Kingdom.

2 (1) Subject to paragraph 3, for the purposes of the first principle personal data are not to be treated as processed fairly unless—

(a) in the case of data obtained from the data subject, the data controller ensures so far as practicable that the data subject has, is provided with, or has made readily available to him, the information specified in sub-paragraph (3), and

(b) in any other case, the data controller ensures so far as practicable that, before the relevant time or as soon as practicable after that time, the data subject has, is provided with, or has made readily available to him, the information specified in sub-paragraph (3).

(2) In sub-paragraph (1)(b) "the relevant time" means—

(a) the time when the data controller first processes the data, or

(b) in a case where at that time disclosure to a third party within a reasonable period is envisaged—

(i) if the data are in fact disclosed to such a person within that period, the time when the data are first disclosed,

(ii) if within that period the data controller becomes, or ought to become, aware that the data are unlikely to be disclosed to such a person within that period, the time when the data controller does become, or ought to become, so aware, or

(iii) in any other case, the end of that period.

(3) The information referred to in sub-paragraph (1) is as follows, namely—

(a) the identity of the data controller,

(b) if he has nominated a representative for the purposes of this Act, the identity of that representative,

(c) the purpose or purposes for which the data are intended to be processed, and

(d) any further information which is necessary, having regard to the specific circumstances in which the data are or are to be processed, to enable processing in respect of the data subject to be fair.

3 (1) Paragraph 2(1)(b) does not apply where either of the primary conditions in sub-paragraph (2), together with such further conditions as may be prescribed by the Secretary of State by order, are met.

(2) The primary conditions referred to in sub-paragraph (1) are—

(a) that the provision of that information would involve a disproportionate effort, or

(b) that the recording of the information to be contained in the data by, or the disclosure of the data by, the data controller is necessary for compliance with any legal obligation to which the data controller is subject, other than an obligation imposed by contract.

4 (1) Personal data which contain a general identifier falling within a description prescribed by the Secretary of State by order are not to be treated as processed fairly and lawfully unless they are processed in compliance with any conditions so prescribed in relation to general identifiers of that description.

(2) In sub-paragraph (1) "a general identifier" means any identifier (such as, for example, a number or code used for identification purposes) which—

(a) relates to an individual, and

(b) forms part of a set of similar identifiers which is of general application.

The second principle

5 The purpose or purposes for which personal data are obtained may in particular be specified—

(a) in a notice given for the purposes of paragraph 2 by the data controller to the data subject, or

(b) in a notification given to the Commissioner under Part III of this Act.

6 In determining whether any disclosure of personal data is compatible with the purpose or purposes for which the data were obtained, regard is to be had to the purpose or purposes for which the personal data are intended to be processed by any person to whom they are disclosed.

The fourth principle

7 The fourth principle is not to be regarded as being contravened by reason of any inaccuracy in personal data which accurately record information obtained by the data controller from the data subject or a third party in a case where—

(a) having regard to the purpose or purposes for which the data were obtained and further processed, the data controller has taken reasonable steps to ensure the accuracy of the data, and

(b) if the data subject has notified the data controller of the data subject's view that the data are inaccurate, the data indicate that fact.

The sixth principle

8 A person is to be regarded as contravening the sixth principle if, but only if—

(a) he contravenes section 7 by failing to supply information in accordance with that section,

(b) he contravenes section 10 by failing to comply with a notice given under subsection (1) of that section to the extent that the notice is justified or by failing to give a notice under subsection (3) of that section,

(c) he contravenes section 11 by failing to comply with a notice given under subsection (1) of that section, or

(d) he contravenes section 12 by failing to comply with a notice given under subsection (1) or (2)(b) of that section or by failing to give a notification under subsection (2)(a) of that section or a notice under subsection (3) of that section.

The seventh principle

9 Having regard to the state of technological development and the cost of implementing any measures, the measures must ensure a level of security appropriate to—

(a) the harm that might result from such unauthorised or unlawful processing or accidental loss, destruction or damage as are mentioned in the seventh principle, and

(b) the nature of the data to be protected.

10 The data controller must take reasonable steps to ensure the reliability of any employees of his who have access to the personal data.

11 Where processing of personal data is carried out by a data processor on behalf of a data controller, the data controller must in order to comply with the seventh principle—

(a) choose a data processor providing sufficient guarantees in respect of the technical and organisational security measures governing the processing to be carried out, and

(b) take reasonable steps to ensure compliance with those measures.

12 Where processing of personal data is carried out by a data processor on behalf of a data controller, the data controller is not to be regarded as complying with the seventh principle unless—

(a) the processing is carried out under a contract—

(i) which is made or evidenced in writing, and

(ii) under which the data processor is to act only on instructions from the data controller, and

(b) the contract requires the data processor to comply with obligations equivalent to those imposed on a data controller by the seventh principle.

The eighth principle

13 An adequate level of protection is one which is adequate in all the circumstances of the case, having regard in particular to—

(a) the nature of the personal data,

(b) the country or territory of origin of the information contained in the data,

(c) the country or territory of final destination of that information,

(d) the purposes for which and period during which the data are intended to be processed,

(e) the law in force in the country or territory in question,

(f) the international obligations of that country or territory,

(g) any relevant codes of conduct or other rules which are enforceable in that country or territory (whether generally or by arrangement in particular cases), and

(h) any security measures taken in respect of the data in that country or territory.

14 The eighth principle does not apply to a transfer falling within any paragraph of Schedule 4, except in such circumstances and to such extent as the Secretary of State may by order provide.

15 (1) Where—

(a) in any proceedings under this Act any question arises as to whether the requirement of the eighth principle as to an adequate level of protection is met in relation to the transfer of any personal data to a country or territory outside the European Economic Area, and

(b) a Community finding has been made in relation to transfers of the kind in question,

that question is to be determined in accordance with that finding.

(2) In sub-paragraph (1) "Community finding" means a finding of the European Commission, under the procedure provided for in Article 31(2) of the Data Protection Directive, that a country or territory outside the European Economic Area does, or does not, ensure an adequate level of protection within the meaning of Article 25(2) of the Directive.

SCHEDULE 2

Section 4(3).

Conditions relevant for purposes of the first principle: processing of any personal data

1 The data subject has given his consent to the processing.

2 The processing is necessary—

(a) for the performance of a contract to which the data subject is a party, or

(b) for the taking of steps at the request of the data subject with a view to entering into a contract.

3 The processing is necessary for compliance with any legal obligation to which the data controller is subject, other than an obligation imposed by contract.

4 The processing is necessary in order to protect the vital interests of the data subject.

5 The processing is necessary—

(a) for the administration of justice,

(b) for the exercise of any functions conferred on any person by or under any enactment,

(c) for the exercise of any functions of the Crown, a Minister of the Crown or a government department, or

(d) for the exercise of any other functions of a public nature exercised in the public interest by any person.

6 (1) The processing is necessary for the purposes of legitimate interests pursued by the data controller or by the third party or parties to whom the data are disclosed, except where the processing is unwarranted in any particular case by reason of prejudice to the rights and freedoms or legitimate interests of the data subject.

(2) The Secretary of State may by order specify particular circumstances in which this condition is, or is not, to be taken to be satisfied.

SCHEDULE 3

Section 4(3).

CONDITIONS RELEVANT FOR PURPOSES OF THE FIRST PRINCIPLE: PROCESSING OF SENSITIVE PERSONAL DATA

1 The data subject has given his explicit consent to the processing of the personal data.

2 (1) The processing is necessary for the purposes of exercising or performing any right or obligation which is conferred or imposed by law on the data controller in connection with employment.

(2) The Secretary of State may by order—

(a) exclude the application of sub-paragraph (1) in such cases as may be specified, or

(b) provide that, in such cases as may be specified, the condition in sub-paragraph (1) is not to be regarded as satisfied unless such further conditions as may be specified in the order are also satisfied.

3 The processing is necessary—

(a) in order to protect the vital interests of the data subject or another person, in a case where—

(i) consent cannot be given by or on behalf of the data subject, or

(ii) the data controller cannot reasonably be expected to obtain the consent of the data subject, or

(b) in order to protect the vital interests of another person, in a case where consent by or on behalf of the data subject has been unreasonably withheld.

4 The processing—

(a) is carried out in the course of its legitimate activities by any body or association which—

(i) is not established or conducted for profit, and

(ii) exists for political, philosophical, religious or trade-union purposes,

(b) is carried out with appropriate safeguards for the rights and freedoms of data subjects,

(c) relates only to individuals who either are members of the body or association or have regular contact with it in connection with its purposes, and

(d) does not involve disclosure of the personal data to a third party without the consent of the data subject.

5 The information contained in the personal data has been made public as a result of steps deliberately taken by the data subject.

6 The processing—

(a) is necessary for the purpose of, or in connection with, any legal proceedings (including prospective legal proceedings),

(b) is necessary for the purpose of obtaining legal advice, or

(c) is otherwise necessary for the purposes of establishing, exercising or defending legal rights.

7 (1) The processing is necessary—

(a) for the administration of justice,

(b) for the exercise of any functions conferred on any person by or under an enactment, or

(c) for the exercise of any functions of the Crown, a Minister of the Crown or a government department.

(2) The Secretary of State may by order—

(a) exclude the application of sub-paragraph (1) in such cases as may be specified, or

(b) provide that, in such cases as may be specified, the condition in sub-paragraph (1) is not to be regarded as satisfied unless such further conditions as may be specified in the order are also satisfied.

8 (1) The processing is necessary for medical purposes and is undertaken by—

(a) a health professional, or

(b) a person who in the circumstances owes a duty of confidentiality which is equivalent to that which would arise if that person were a health professional.

(2) In this paragraph "medical purposes" includes the purposes of preventative medicine, medical diagnosis, medical research, the provision of care and treatment and the management of healthcare services.

9 (1) The processing—

(a) is of sensitive personal data consisting of information as to racial or ethnic origin,

(b) is necessary for the purpose of identifying or keeping under review the existence or absence of equality of opportunity or treatment between persons of different racial or ethnic origins, with a view to enabling such equality to be promoted or maintained, and

(c) is carried out with appropriate safeguards for the rights and freedoms of data subjects.

(2) The Secretary of State may by order specify circumstances in which processing falling within sub-paragraph (1)(a) and (b) is, or is not, to be taken for the purposes of sub-paragraph (1)(c) to be carried out with appropriate safeguards for the rights and freedoms of data subjects.

10 The personal data are processed in circumstances specified in an order made by the Secretary of State for the purposes of this paragraph.

SCHEDULE 4

Section 4(3).

Cases where the eighth principle does not apply

1 The data subject has given his consent to the transfer.

2 The transfer is necessary—

(a) for the performance of a contract between the data subject and the data controller, or

(b) for the taking of steps at the request of the data subject with a view to his entering into a contract with the data controller.

3 The transfer is necessary—

(a) for the conclusion of a contract between the data controller and a person other than the data subject which—

(i) is entered into at the request of the data subject, or

(ii) is in the interests of the data subject, or

(b) for the performance of such a contract.

4 (1) The transfer is necessary for reasons of substantial public interest.

(2) The Secretary of State may by order specify—

(a) circumstances in which a transfer is to be taken for the purposes of sub-paragraph (1) to be necessary for reasons of substantial public interest, and

(b) circumstances in which a transfer which is not required by or under an enactment is not to be taken for the purpose of sub-paragraph (1) to be necessary for reasons of substantial public interest.

5 The transfer—

(a) is necessary for the purpose of, or in connection with, any legal proceedings (including prospective legal proceedings),

(b) is necessary for the purpose of obtaining legal advice, or

(c) is otherwise necessary for the purposes of establishing, exercising or defending legal rights.

6 The transfer is necessary in order to protect the vital interests of the data subject.

7 The transfer is of part of the personal data on a public register and any conditions subject to which the register is open to inspection are complied with by any person to whom the data are or may be disclosed after the transfer.

8 The transfer is made on terms which are of a kind approved by the Commissioner as ensuring adequate safeguards for the rights and freedoms of data subjects.

9 The transfer has been authorised by the Commissioner as being made in such a manner as to ensure adequate safeguards for the rights and freedoms of data subjects.

SCHEDULE 5

Section 6(7).

THE DATA PROTECTION COMMISSIONER AND THE DATA PROTECTION TRIBUNAL

PART I

THE COMMISSIONER

Status and capacity

1 (1) The corporation sole by the name of the Data Protection Registrar established by the Data Protection Act 1984 shall continue in existence by the name of the Data Protection Commissioner.

(2) The Commissioner and his officers and staff are not to be regarded as servants or agents of the Crown.

Tenure of office

2 (1) Subject to the provisions of this paragraph, the Commissioner shall hold office for such term not exceeding five years as may be determined at the time of his appointment.

(2) The Commissioner may be relieved of his office by Her Majesty at his own request.

(3) The Commissioner may be removed from office by Her Majesty in pursuance of an Address from both Houses of Parliament.

(4) The Commissioner shall in any case vacate his office—

(a) on completing the year of service in which he attains the age of sixty-five years, or

(b) if earlier, on completing his fifteenth year of service.

(5) Subject to sub-paragraph (4), a person who ceases to be Commissioner on the expiration of his term of office shall be eligible for re-appointment, but a person may not be re-appointed for a third or subsequent term as Commissioner unless, by reason of special circumstances, the person's re-appointment for such a term is desirable in the public interest.

Salary etc.

3 (1) There shall be paid—

(a) to the Commissioner such salary, and

(b) to or in respect of the Commissioner such pension,

as may be specified by a resolution of the House of Commons.

(2) A resolution for the purposes of this paragraph may—

(a) specify the salary or pension,

(b) provide that the salary or pension is to be the same as, or calculated on the same basis as, that payable to, or to or in respect of, a person employed in a specified office under, or in a specified capacity in the service of, the Crown, or

(c) specify the salary or pension and provide for it to be increased by reference to such variables as may be specified in the resolution.

(3) A resolution for the purposes of this paragraph may take effect from the date on which it is passed or from any earlier or later date specified in the resolution.

(4) A resolution for the purposes of this paragraph may make different provision in relation to the pension payable to or in respect of different holders of the office of Commissioner.

(5) Any salary or pension payable under this paragraph shall be charged on and issued out of the Consolidated Fund.

(6) In this paragraph "pension" includes an allowance or gratuity and any reference to the payment of a pension includes a reference to the making of payments towards the provision of a pension.

Officers and staff

4 (1) The Commissioner—

(a) shall appoint a deputy commissioner, and
(b) may appoint such number of other officers and staff as he may determine.

(2) The remuneration and other conditions of service of the persons appointed under this paragraph shall be determined by the Commissioner.

(3) The Commissioner may pay such pensions, allowances or gratuities to or in respect of the persons appointed under this paragraph, or make such payments towards the provision of such pensions, allowances or gratuities, as he may determine.

(4) The references in sub-paragraph (3) to pensions, allowances or gratuities to or in respect of the persons appointed under this paragraph include references to pensions, allowances or gratuities by way of compensation to or in respect of any of those persons who suffer loss of office or employment.

(5) Any determination under sub-paragraph (1)(b), (2) or (3) shall require the approval of the Secretary of State.

(6) The Employers' Liability (Compulsory Insurance) Act 1969 shall not require insurance to be effected by the Commissioner.

5 (1) The deputy commissioner shall perform the functions conferred by this Act on the Commissioner during any vacancy in that office or at any time when the Commissioner is for any reason unable to act.

(2) Without prejudice to sub-paragraph (1), any functions of the Commissioner under this Act may, to the extent authorised by him, be performed by any of his officers or staff.

Authentication of seal of the Commissioner

6 The application of the seal of the Commissioner shall be authenticated by his signature or by the signature of some other person authorised for the purpose.

Presumption of authenticity of documents issued by the Commissioner

7 Any document purporting to be an instrument issued by the Commissioner and to be duly executed under the Commissioner's seal or to be signed by or on behalf of the Commissioner shall be received in evidence and shall be deemed to be such an instrument unless the contrary is shown.

Money

8 The Secretary of State may make payments to the Commissioner out of money provided by Parliament.

9 (1) All fees and other sums received by the Commissioner in the exercise of his functions under this Act or section 159 of the Consumer Credit Act 1974 shall be paid by him to the Secretary of State.

(2) Sub-paragraph (1) shall not apply where the Secretary of State, with the consent of the Treasury, otherwise directs.

(3) Any sums received by the Secretary of State under sub-paragraph (1) shall be paid into the Consolidated Fund.

Accounts

10 (1) It shall be the duty of the Commissioner—

(a) to keep proper accounts and other records in relation to the accounts,

(b) to prepare in respect of each financial year a statement of account in such form as the Secretary of State may direct, and

(c) to send copies of that statement to the Comptroller and Auditor General on or before 31st August next following the end of the year to which the statement relates or on or before such earlier date after the end of that year as the Treasury may direct.

(2) The Comptroller and Auditor General shall examine and certify any statement sent to him under this paragraph and lay copies of it together with his report thereon before each House of Parliament.

(3) In this paragraph "financial year" means a period of twelve months beginning with 1st April.

Application of Part I in Scotland

11 Paragraphs 1(1), 6 and 7 do not extend to Scotland.

Part II

The Tribunal

Tenure of office

12 (1) Subject to the following provisions of this paragraph, a member of the Tribunal shall hold and vacate his office in accordance with the terms of his appointment and shall, on ceasing to hold office, be eligible for re-appointment.

(2) Any member of the Tribunal may at any time resign his office by notice in writing to the Lord Chancellor (in the case of the chairman or a deputy chairman) or to the Secretary of State (in the case of any other member).

(3) A person who is the chairman or deputy chairman of the Tribunal shall vacate his office on the day on which he attains the age of seventy years; but this sub-paragraph is subject to section 26(4) to (6) of the Judicial Pensions and Retirement Act 1993 (power to authorise continuance in office up to the age of seventy-five years).

Salary etc.

13 The Secretary of State shall pay to the members of the Tribunal out of money provided by Parliament such remuneration and allowances as he may determine.

Officers and staff

14 The Secretary of State may provide the Tribunal with such officers and staff as he thinks necessary for the proper discharge of its functions.

Expenses

15 Such expenses of the Tribunal as the Secretary of State may determine shall be defrayed by the Secretary of State out of money provided by Parliament.

PART III

TRANSITIONAL PROVISIONS

16 Any reference in any enactment, instrument or other document to the Data Protection Registrar shall be construed, in relation to any time after the commencement of section 6(1), as a reference to the Commissioner.

17 Any reference in this Act or in any instrument under this Act to the Commissioner shall be construed, in relation to any time before the commencement of section 6(1), as a reference to the Data Protection Registrar.

SCHEDULE 6

Sections 28(12), 48(5).

APPEAL PROCEEDINGS

Hearing of appeals

1 For the purpose of hearing and determining appeals or any matter preliminary or incidental to an appeal the Tribunal shall sit at such times and in such places as the chairman or a deputy chairman may direct and may sit in two or more divisions.

Constitution of Tribunal in national security cases

2 (1) The Lord Chancellor shall from time to time designate, from among the chairman and deputy chairmen appointed by him under section 6(4)(a) and (b), those persons who are to be capable of hearing appeals under section 28(4) or (6).

(2) A designation under sub-paragraph (1) may at any time be revoked by the Lord Chancellor.

3 In any case where the application of paragraph 6(1) is excluded by rules under paragraph 7, the Tribunal shall be duly constituted for an appeal under section 28(4) or (6) if it consists of three of the persons designated under paragraph 2(1), of whom one shall be designated by the Lord Chancellor to preside.

Constitution of Tribunal in other cases

4 (1) Subject to any rules made under paragraph 7, the Tribunal shall be duly constituted for an appeal under section 48(1), (2) or (4) if it consists of—

(a) the chairman or a deputy chairman (who shall preside), and

(b) an equal number of the members appointed respectively in accordance with paragraphs (a) and (b) of section 6(6).

(2) The members who are to constitute the Tribunal in accordance with sub-paragraph (1) shall be nominated by the chairman or, if he is for any reason unable to act, by a deputy chairman.

Determination of questions by full Tribunal

5 The determination of any question before the Tribunal when constituted in accordance with paragraph 3 or 4 shall be according to the opinion of the majority of the members hearing the appeal.

Ex parte proceedings

6 (1) Subject to any rules made under paragraph 7, the jurisdiction of the Tribunal in respect of an appeal under section 28(4) or (6) shall be exercised ex parte by one or more persons designated under paragraph 2(1).

(2) Subject to any rules made under paragraph 7, the jurisdiction of the Tribunal in respect of an appeal under section 48(3) shall be exercised ex parte by the chairman or a deputy chairman sitting alone.

Rules of procedure

7 (1) The Secretary of State may make rules for regulating the exercise of the rights of appeal conferred by sections 28(4) or (6) and 48 and the practice and procedure of the Tribunal.

(2) Rules under this paragraph may in particular make provision—

(a) with respect to the period within which an appeal can be brought and the burden of proof on an appeal,

(b) for the summoning (or, in Scotland, citation) of witnesses and the administration of oaths,

(c) for securing the production of documents and material used for the processing of personal data,

(d) for the inspection, examination, operation and testing of any equipment or material used in connection with the processing of personal data,

(e) for the hearing of an appeal wholly or partly in camera,

(f) for hearing an appeal in the absence of the appellant or for determining an appeal without a hearing,

(g) for enabling an appeal under section 48(1) against an information notice to be determined by the chairman or a deputy chairman,

(h) for enabling any matter preliminary or incidental to an appeal to be dealt with by the chairman or a deputy chairman,

(i) for the awarding of costs or, in Scotland, expenses,

(j) for the publication of reports of the Tribunal's decisions, and

(k) for conferring on the Tribunal such ancillary powers as the Secretary of State thinks necessary for the proper discharge of its functions.

(3) In making rules under this paragraph which relate to appeals under section 28(4) or (6) the Secretary of State shall have regard, in particular, to the need to secure that information is not disclosed contrary to the public interest.

Obstruction etc.

8 (1) If any person is guilty of any act or omission in relation to proceedings before the Tribunal which, if those proceedings were proceedings before a court having power

to commit for contempt, would constitute contempt of court, the Tribunal may certify the offence to the High Court or, in Scotland, the Court of Session.

(2) Where an offence is so certified, the court may inquire into the matter and, after hearing any witness who may be produced against or on behalf of the person charged with the offence, and after hearing any statement that may be offered in defence, deal with him in any manner in which it could deal with him if he had committed the like offence in relation to the court.

SCHEDULE 7

Section 37.

MISCELLANEOUS EXEMPTIONS

Confidential references given by the data controller

1 Personal data are exempt from section 7 if they consist of a reference given or to be given in confidence by the data controller for the purposes of—

- (a) the education, training or employment, or prospective education, training or employment, of the data subject,
- (b) the appointment, or prospective appointment, of the data subject to any office, or
- (c) the provision, or prospective provision, by the data subject of any service.

Armed forces

2 Personal data are exempt from the subject information provisions in any case to the extent to which the application of those provisions would be likely to prejudice the combat effectiveness of any of the armed forces of the Crown.

Judicial appointments and honours

3 Personal data processed for the purposes of—

- (a) assessing any person's suitability for judicial office or the office of Queen's Counsel, or
- (b) the conferring by the Crown of any honour,

are exempt from the subject information provisions.

Crown employment and Crown or Ministerial appointments

4 The Secretary of State may by order exempt from the subject information provisions personal data processed for the purposes of assessing any person's suitability for—

- (a) employment by or under the Crown, or
- (b) any office to which appointments are made by Her Majesty, by a Minister of the Crown or by a Northern Ireland department.

Management forecasts etc.

5 Personal data processed for the purposes of management forecasting or management planning to assist the data controller in the conduct of any business or other activity are exempt from the subject information provisions in any case to the

extent to which the application of those provisions would be likely to prejudice the conduct of that business or other activity.

Corporate finance

6 (1) Where personal data are processed for the purposes of, or in connection with, a corporate finance service provided by a relevant person—

(a) the data are exempt from the subject information provisions in any case to the extent to which either—

(i) the application of those provisions to the data could affect the price of any instrument which is already in existence or is to be or may be created, or

(ii) the data controller reasonably believes that the application of those provisions to the data could affect the price of any such instrument, and

(b) to the extent that the data are not exempt from the subject information provisions by virtue of paragraph (a), they are exempt from those provisions if the exemption is required for the purpose of safeguarding an important economic or financial interest of the United Kingdom.

(2) For the purposes of sub-paragraph (1)(b) the Secretary of State may by order specify—

(a) matters to be taken into account in determining whether exemption from the subject information provisions is required for the purpose of safeguarding an important economic or financial interest of the United Kingdom, or

(b) circumstances in which exemption from those provisions is, or is not, to be taken to be required for that purpose.

(3) In this paragraph—

"corporate finance service" means a service consisting in—

(a) underwriting in respect of issues of, or the placing of issues of, any instrument,

(b) advice to undertakings on capital structure, industrial strategy and related matters and advice and service relating to mergers and the purchase of undertakings, or

(c) services relating to such underwriting as is mentioned in paragraph (a);

"instrument" means any instrument listed in section B of the Annex to the Council Directive on investment services in the securities field (93/22/EEC), as set out in Schedule 1 to the Investment Services Regulations 1995;

"price" includes value;

"relevant person" means—

(a) any person who is authorised under Chapter III of Part I of the Financial Services Act 1986 or is an exempted person under Chapter IV of Part I of that Act,

(b) any person who, but for Part III or IV of Schedule 1 to that Act, would require authorisation under that Act,

(c) any European investment firm within the meaning given by Regulation 3 of the Investment Services Regulations 1995,

(d) any person who, in the course of his employment, provides to his employer a service falling within paragraph (b) or (c) of the definition of "corporate finance service", or

(e) any partner who provides to other partners in the partnership a service falling within either of those paragraphs.

Negotiations

7 Personal data which consist of records of the intentions of the data controller in relation to any negotiations with the data subject are exempt from the subject information provisions in any case to the extent to which the application of those provisions would be likely to prejudice those negotiations.

Examination marks

8 (1) Section 7 shall have effect subject to the provisions of sub-paragraphs (2) to (4) in the case of personal data consisting of marks or other information processed by a data controller—

(a) for the purpose of determining the results of an academic, professional or other examination or of enabling the results of any such examination to be determined, or

(b) in consequence of the determination of any such results.

(2) Where the relevant day falls before the day on which the results of the examination are announced, the period mentioned in section 7(8) shall be extended until—

(a) the end of five months beginning with the relevant day, or

(b) the end of forty days beginning with the date of the announcement,

whichever is the earlier.

(3) Where by virtue of sub-paragraph (2) a period longer than the prescribed period elapses after the relevant day before the request is complied with, the information to be supplied pursuant to the request shall be supplied both by reference to the data in question at the time when the request is received and (if different) by reference to the data as from time to time held in the period beginning when the request is received and ending when it is complied with.

(4) For the purposes of this paragraph the results of an examination shall be treated as announced when they are first published or (if not published) when they are first made available or communicated to the candidate in question.

(5) In this paragraph—

"examination" includes any process for determining the knowledge, intelligence, skill or ability of a candidate by reference to his performance in any test, work or other activity;

"the prescribed period" means forty days or such other period as is for the time being prescribed under section 7 in relation to the personal data in question;

"relevant day" has the same meaning as in section 7.

Examination scripts etc.

9 (1) Personal data consisting of information recorded by candidates during an academic, professional or other examination are exempt from section 7.

(2) In this paragraph "examination" has the same meaning as in paragraph 8.

Legal professional privilege

10 Personal data are exempt from the subject information provisions if the data consist of information in respect of which a claim to legal professional privilege or, in Scotland, to confidentiality as between client and professional legal adviser, could be maintained in legal proceedings.

Self-incrimination

11 (1) A person need not comply with any request or order under section 7 to the extent that compliance would, by revealing evidence of the commission of any offence other than an offence under this Act, expose him to proceedings for that offence.

(2) Information disclosed by any person in compliance with any request or order under section 7 shall not be admissible against him in proceedings for an offence under this Act.

SCHEDULE 8

Section 39.

TRANSITIONAL RELIEF

PART I

INTERPRETATION OF SCHEDULE

1 (1) For the purposes of this Schedule, personal data are "eligible data" at any time if, and to the extent that, they are at that time subject to processing which was already under way immediately before 24th October 1998.

(2) In this Schedule—

"eligible automated data" means eligible data which fall within paragraph (a) or (b) of the definition of "data" in section 1(1);

"eligible manual data" means eligible data which are not eligible automated data;

"the first transitional period" means the period beginning with the commencement of this Schedule and ending with 23rd October 2001;

"the second transitional period" means the period beginning with 24th October 2001 and ending with 23rd October 2007.

PART II

EXEMPTIONS AVAILABLE BEFORE 24TH OCTOBER 2001

Manual data

2 (1) Eligible manual data, other than data forming part of an accessible record, are exempt from the data protection principles and Parts II and III of this Act during the first transitional period.

(2) This paragraph does not apply to eligible manual data to which paragraph 4 applies.

3 (1) This paragraph applies to—
(a) eligible manual data forming part of an accessible record, and
(b) personal data which fall within paragraph (d) of the definition of "data" in section 1(1) but which, because they are not subject to processing which was already under way immediately before 24th October 1998, are not eligible data for the purposes of this Schedule.

(2) During the first transitional period, data to which this paragraph applies are exempt from—
(a) the data protection principles, except the sixth principle so far as relating to sections 7 and 12A,
(b) Part II of this Act, except—
(i) section 7 (as it has effect subject to section 8) and section 12A, and
(ii) section 15 so far as relating to those sections, and
(c) Part III of this Act.

4 (1) This paragraph applies to eligible manual data which consist of information relevant to the financial standing of the data subject and in respect of which the data controller is a credit reference agency.

(2) During the first transitional period, data to which this paragraph applies are exempt from—
(a) the data protection principles, except the sixth principle so far as relating to sections 7 and 12A,
(b) Part II of this Act, except—
(i) section 7 (as it has effect subject to sections 8 and 9) and section 12A, and
(ii) section 15 so far as relating to those sections, and
(c) Part III of this Act.

Processing otherwise than by reference to the data subject

5 During the first transitional period, for the purposes of this Act (apart from paragraph 1), eligible automated data are not to be regarded as being "processed" unless the processing is by reference to the data subject.

Payrolls and accounts

6 (1) Subject to sub-paragraph (2), eligible automated data processed by a data controller for one or more of the following purposes—
(a) calculating amounts payable by way of remuneration or pensions in respect of service in any employment or office or making payments of, or of sums deducted from, such remuneration or pensions, or
(b) keeping accounts relating to any business or other activity carried on by the data controller or keeping records of purchases, sales or other transactions for the purpose of ensuring that the requisite payments are made by or to him in respect of those transactions or for the purpose of making financial or management forecasts to assist him in the conduct of any such business or activity,

are exempt from the data protection principles and Parts II and III of this Act during the first transitional period.

(2) It shall be a condition of the exemption of any eligible automated data under this paragraph that the data are not processed for any other purpose, but the exemption is not lost by any processing of the eligible data for any other purpose if the data controller shows that he had taken such care to prevent it as in all the circumstances was reasonably required.

(3) Data processed only for one or more of the purposes mentioned in sub-paragraph (1) (a) may be disclosed—

(a) to any person, other than the data controller, by whom the remuneration or pensions in question are payable,

(b) for the purpose of obtaining actuarial advice,

(c) for the purpose of giving information as to the persons in any employment or office for use in medical research into the health of, or injuries suffered by, persons engaged in particular occupations or working in particular places or areas,

(d) if the data subject (or a person acting on his behalf) has requested or consented to the disclosure of the data either generally or in the circumstances in which the disclosure in question is made, or

(e) if the person making the disclosure has reasonable grounds for believing that the disclosure falls within paragraph (d).

(4) Data processed for any of the purposes mentioned in sub-paragraph (1) may be disclosed—

(a) for the purpose of audit or where the disclosure is for the purpose only of giving information about the data controller's financial affairs, or

(b) in any case in which disclosure would be permitted by any other provision of this Part of this Act if sub-paragraph (2) were included among the non-disclosure provisions.

(5) In this paragraph "remuneration" includes remuneration in kind and "pensions" includes gratuities or similar benefits.

Unincorporated members' clubs and mailing lists

7 Eligible automated data processed by an unincorporated members' club and relating only to the members of the club are exempt from the data protection principles and Parts II and III of this Act during the first transitional period.

8 Eligible automated data processed by a data controller only for the purposes of distributing, or recording the distribution of, articles or information to the data subjects and consisting only of their names, addresses or other particulars necessary for effecting the distribution, are exempt from the data protection principles and Parts II and III of this Act during the first transitional period.

9 Neither paragraph 7 nor paragraph 8 applies to personal data relating to any data subject unless he has been asked by the club or data controller whether he objects to the data relating to him being processed as mentioned in that paragraph and has not objected.

10 It shall be a condition of the exemption of any data under paragraph 7 that the data are not disclosed except as permitted by paragraph 11 and of the exemption under paragraph 8 that the data are not processed for any purpose other than that mentioned in that paragraph or as permitted by paragraph 11, but—

(a) the exemption under paragraph 7 shall not be lost by any disclosure in breach of that condition, and
(b) the exemption under paragraph 8 shall not be lost by any processing in breach of that condition,

if the data controller shows that he had taken such care to prevent it as in all the circumstances was reasonably required.

11 Data to which paragraph 10 applies may be disclosed—
(a) if the data subject (or a person acting on his behalf) has requested or consented to the disclosure of the data either generally or in the circumstances in which the disclosure in question is made,
(b) if the person making the disclosure has reasonable grounds for believing that the disclosure falls within paragraph (a), or
(c) in any case in which disclosure would be permitted by any other provision of this Part of this Act if paragraph 8 were included among the non-disclosure provisions.

Back-up data

12 Eligible automated data which are processed only for the purpose of replacing other data in the event of the latter being lost, destroyed or impaired are exempt from section 7 during the first transitional period.

Exemption of all eligible automated data from certain requirements

13 (1) During the first transitional period, eligible automated data are exempt from the following provisions—
(a) the first data protection principle to the extent to which it requires compliance with—
(i) paragraph 2 of Part II of Schedule 1,
(ii) the conditions in Schedule 2, and
(iii) the conditions in Schedule 3,
(b) the seventh data protection principle to the extent to which it requires compliance with paragraph 12 of Part II of Schedule 1;
(c) the eighth data protection principle,
(d) in section 7(1), paragraphs (b), (c)(ii) and (d),
(e) sections 10 and 11,
(f) section 12, and
(g) section 13, except so far as relating to—
(i) any contravention of the fourth data protection principle,
(ii) any disclosure without the consent of the data controller,
(iii) loss or destruction of data without the consent of the data controller, or
(iv) processing for the special purposes.

(2) The specific exemptions conferred by sub-paragraph (1)(a), (c) and (e) do not limit the data controller's general duty under the first data protection principle to ensure that processing is fair.

PART III

EXEMPTIONS AVAILABLE AFTER 23RD OCTOBER 2001 BUT BEFORE 24TH OCTOBER 2007

14 (1) This paragraph applies to—

(a) eligible manual data which were held immediately before 24th October 1998, and

(b) personal data which fall within paragraph (d) of the definition of "data" in section 1(1) but do not fall within paragraph (a) of this sub-paragraph,

but does not apply to eligible manual data to which the exemption in paragraph 16 applies.

(2) During the second transitional period, data to which this paragraph applies are exempt from the following provisions—

(a) the first data protection principle except to the extent to which it requires compliance with paragraph 2 of Part II of Schedule 1,

(b) the second, third, fourth and fifth data protection principles, and

(c) section 14(1) to (3).

PART IV

EXEMPTIONS AFTER 23RD OCTOBER 2001 FOR HISTORICAL RESEARCH

15 In this Part of this Schedule "the relevant conditions" has the same meaning as in section 33.

16 (1) Eligible manual data which are processed only for the purpose of historical research in compliance with the relevant conditions are exempt from the provisions specified in sub-paragraph (2) after 23rd October 2001.

(2) The provisions referred to in sub-paragraph (1) are—

(a) the first data protection principle except in so far as it requires compliance with paragraph 2 of Part II of Schedule 1,

(b) the second, third, fourth and fifth data protection principles, and

(c) section 14(1) to (3).

17 (1) After 23rd October 2001 eligible automated data which are processed only for the purpose of historical research in compliance with the relevant conditions are exempt from the first data protection principle to the extent to which it requires compliance with the conditions in Schedules 2 and 3.

(2) Eligible automated data which are processed—

(a) only for the purpose of historical research,

(b) in compliance with the relevant conditions, and

(c) otherwise than by reference to the data subject,

are also exempt from the provisions referred to in sub-paragraph (3) after 23rd October 2001.

(3) The provisions referred to in sub-paragraph (2) are—

(a) the first data protection principle except in so far as it requires compliance with paragraph 2 of Part II of Schedule 1,

(b) the second, third, fourth and fifth data protection principles, and

(c) section 14(1) to (3).

18 For the purposes of this Part of this Schedule personal data are not to be treated as processed otherwise than for the purpose of historical research merely because the data are disclosed—

(a) to any person, for the purpose of historical research only,

(b) to the data subject or a person acting on his behalf,

(c) at the request, or with the consent, of the data subject or a person acting on his behalf, or

(d) in circumstances in which the person making the disclosure has reasonable grounds for believing that the disclosure falls within paragraph (a), (b) or (c).

PART V

EXEMPTION FROM SECTION 22

19 Processing which was already under way immediately before 24th October 1998 is not assessable processing for the purposes of section 22.

SCHEDULE 9

Section 50.

POWERS OF ENTRY AND INSPECTION

Issue of warrants

1 (1) If a circuit judge is satisfied by information on oath supplied by the Commissioner that there are reasonable grounds for suspecting—

(a) that a data controller has contravened or is contravening any of the data protection principles, or

(b) that an offence under this Act has been or is being committed,

and that evidence of the contravention or of the commission of the offence is to be found on any premises specified in the information, he may, subject to sub-paragraph (2) and paragraph 2, grant a warrant to the Commissioner.

(2) A judge shall not issue a warrant under this Schedule in respect of any personal data processed for the special purposes unless a determination by the Commissioner under section 45 with respect to those data has taken effect.

(3) A warrant issued under sub-paragraph (1) shall authorise the Commissioner or any of his officers or staff at any time within seven days of the date of the warrant to enter the premises, to search them, to inspect, examine, operate and test any equipment found there which is used or intended to be used for the processing of personal data and to inspect and seize any documents or other material found there which may be such evidence as is mentioned in that sub-paragraph.

2 (1) A judge shall not issue a warrant under this Schedule unless he is satisfied—

(a) that the Commissioner has given seven days' notice in writing to the occupier of the premises in question demanding access to the premises, and

(b) that either—

(i) access was demanded at a reasonable hour and was unreasonably refused, or

(ii) although entry to the premises was granted, the occupier unreasonably refused to comply with a request by the Commissioner or any of the Commissioner's officers or staff to permit the Commissioner or the officer or member of staff to do any of the things referred to in paragraph 1(3), and

(c) that the occupier, has, after the refusal, been notified by the Commissioner of the application for the warrant and has had an opportunity of being heard by the judge on the question whether or not it should be issued.

(2) Sub-paragraph (1) shall not apply if the judge is satisfied that the case is one of urgency or that compliance with those provisions would defeat the object of the entry.

3 A judge who issues a warrant under this Schedule shall also issue two copies of it and certify them clearly as copies.

Execution of warrants

4 A person executing a warrant issued under this Schedule may use such reasonable force as may be necessary.

5 A warrant issued under this Schedule shall be executed at a reasonable hour unless it appears to the person executing it that there are grounds for suspecting that the evidence in question would not be found if it were so executed.

6 If the person who occupies the premises in respect of which a warrant is issued under this Schedule is present when the warrant is executed, he shall be shown the warrant and supplied with a copy of it; and if that person is not present a copy of the warrant shall be left in a prominent place on the premises.

7 (1) A person seizing anything in pursuance of a warrant under this Schedule shall give a receipt for it if asked to do so.

(2) Anything so seized may be retained for so long as is necessary in all the circumstances but the person in occupation of the premises in question shall be given a copy of anything that is seized if he so requests and the person executing the warrant considers that it can be done without undue delay.

Matters exempt from inspection and seizure

8 The powers of inspection and seizure conferred by a warrant issued under this Schedule shall not be exercisable in respect of personal data which by virtue of section 28 are exempt from any of the provisions of this Act.

9 (1) Subject to the provisions of this paragraph, the powers of inspection and seizure conferred by a warrant issued under this Schedule shall not be exercisable in respect of—

(a) any communication between a professional legal adviser and his client in connection with the giving of legal advice to the client with respect to his obligations, liabilities or rights under this Act, or

(b) any communication between a professional legal adviser and his client, or between such an adviser or his client and any other person, made in connection with or in contemplation of proceedings under or arising out of this Act (including proceedings before the Tribunal) and for the purposes of such proceedings.

(2) Sub-paragraph (1) applies also to—

(a) any copy or other record of any such communication as is there mentioned, and

(b) any document or article enclosed with or referred to in any such communication if made in connection with the giving of any advice or, as the case may be, in connection with or in contemplation of and for the purposes of such proceedings as are there mentioned.

(3) This paragraph does not apply to anything in the possession of any person other than the professional legal adviser or his client or to anything held with the intention of furthering a criminal purpose.

(4) In this paragraph references to the client of a professional legal adviser include references to any person representing such a client.

10 If the person in occupation of any premises in respect of which a warrant is issued under this Schedule objects to the inspection or seizure under the warrant of any material on the grounds that it consists partly of matters in respect of which those powers are not exercisable, he shall, if the person executing the warrant so requests, furnish that person with a copy of so much of the material as is not exempt from those powers.

Return of warrants

11 A warrant issued under this Schedule shall be returned to the court from which it was issued—

(a) after being executed, or

(b) if not executed within the time authorised for its execution;

and the person by whom any such warrant is executed shall make an endorsement on it stating what powers have been exercised by him under the warrant.

Offences

12 Any person who—

(a) intentionally obstructs a person in the execution of a warrant issued under this Schedule, or

(b) fails without reasonable excuse to give any person executing such a warrant such assistance as he may reasonably require for the execution of the warrant,

is guilty of an offence.

Vessels, vehicles etc.

13 In this Schedule "premises" includes any vessel, vehicle, aircraft or hovercraft, and references to the occupier of any premises include references to the person in charge of any vessel, vehicle, aircraft or hovercraft.

Scotland and Northern Ireland

14 In the application of this Schedule to Scotland—

(a) for any reference to a circuit judge there is substituted a reference to the sheriff,

(b) for any reference to information on oath there is substituted a reference to evidence on oath, and

(c) for the reference to the court from which the warrant was issued there is substituted a reference to the sheriff clerk.

15 In the application of this Schedule to Northern Ireland—

(a) for any reference to a circuit judge there is substituted a reference to a county court judge, and

(b) for any reference to information on oath there is substituted a reference to a complaint on oath.

SCHEDULE 10

Section 53(6).

FURTHER PROVISIONS RELATING TO ASSISTANCE UNDER SECTION 53

1 In this Schedule "applicant" and "proceedings" have the same meaning as in section 53.

2 The assistance provided under section 53 may include the making of arrangements for, or for the Commissioner to bear the costs of—

(a) the giving of advice or assistance by a solicitor or counsel, and

(b) the representation of the applicant, or the provision to him of such assistance as is usually given by a solicitor or counsel—

(i) in steps preliminary or incidental to the proceedings, or

(ii) in arriving at or giving effect to a compromise to avoid or bring an end to the proceedings.

3 Where assistance is provided with respect to the conduct of proceedings—

(a) it shall include an agreement by the Commissioner to indemnify the applicant (subject only to any exceptions specified in the notification) in respect of any liability to pay costs or expenses arising by virtue of any judgment or order of the court in the proceedings,

(b) it may include an agreement by the Commissioner to indemnify the applicant in respect of any liability to pay costs or expenses arising by virtue of any compromise or settlement arrived at in order to avoid the proceedings or bring the proceedings to an end, and

(c) it may include an agreement by the Commissioner to indemnify the applicant in respect of any liability to pay damages pursuant to an undertaking given on the grant of interlocutory relief (in Scotland, an interim order) to the applicant.

4 Where the Commissioner provides assistance in relation to any proceedings, he shall do so on such terms, or make such other arrangements, as will secure that a person against whom the proceedings have been or are commenced is informed that assistance has been or is being provided by the Commissioner in relation to them.

5 In England and Wales or Northern Ireland, the recovery of expenses incurred by the Commissioner in providing an applicant with assistance (as taxed or assessed in such manner as may be prescribed by rules of court) shall constitute a first charge for the benefit of the Commissioner—

(a) on any costs which, by virtue of any judgment or order of the court, are payable to the applicant by any other person in respect of the matter in connection with which the assistance is provided, and
(b) on any sum payable to the applicant under a compromise or settlement arrived at in connection with that matter to avoid or bring to an end any proceedings.

6 In Scotland, the recovery of such expenses (as taxed or assessed in such manner as may be prescribed by rules of court) shall be paid to the Commissioner, in priority to other debts—
(a) out of any expenses which, by virtue of any judgment or order of the court, are payable to the applicant by any other person in respect of the matter in connection with which the assistance is provided, and
(b) out of any sum payable to the applicant under a compromise or settlement arrived at in connection with that matter to avoid or bring to an end any proceedings.

SCHEDULE 11

Section 68(1)(6).

EDUCATIONAL RECORDS

Meaning of "educational record"

1 For the purposes of section 68 "educational record" means any record to which paragraph 2, 5 or 7 applies.

England and Wales

2 This paragraph applies to any record of information which—
(a) is processed by or on behalf of the governing body of, or a teacher at, any school in England and Wales specified in paragraph 3,
(b) relates to any person who is or has been a pupil at the school, and
(c) originated from or was supplied by or on behalf of any of the persons specified in paragraph 4,

other than information which is processed by a teacher solely for the teacher's own use.

3 The schools referred to in paragraph 2(a) are—
(a) a school maintained by a local education authority, and
(b) a special school, as defined by section 6(2) of the Education Act 1996, which is not so maintained.

4 The persons referred to in paragraph 2(c) are—
(a) an employee of the local education authority which maintains the school,
(b) in the case of—
(i) a voluntary aided, foundation or foundation special school (within the meaning of the School Standards and Framework Act 1998), or
(ii) a special school which is not maintained by a local eduction authority,

a teacher or other employee at the school (including an educational psychologist engaged by the governing body under a contract for services),

(c) the pupil to whom the record relates, and

(d) a parent, as defined by section 576(1) of the Education Act 1996, of that pupil.

Scotland

5 This paragraph applies to any record of information which is processed—

(a) by an education authority in Scotland, and

(b) for the purpose of the relevant function of the authority,

other than information which is processed by a teacher solely for the teacher's own use.

6 For the purposes of paragraph 5—

(a) "education authority" means an education authority within the meaning of the Education (Scotland) Act 1980 ("the 1980 Act") or, in relation to a self-governing school, the board of management within the meaning of the Self-Governing Schools etc. (Scotland) Act 1989 ("the 1989 Act"),

(b) "the relevant function" means, in relation to each of those authorities, their function under section 1 of the 1980 Act and section 7(1) of the 1989 Act, and

(c) information processed by an education authority is processed for the purpose of the relevant function of the authority if the processing relates to the discharge of that function in respect of a person—

(i) who is or has been a pupil in a school provided by the authority, or

(ii) who receives, or has received, further education (within the meaning of the 1980 Act) so provided.

Northern Ireland

7 (1) This paragraph applies to any record of information which—

(a) is processed by or on behalf of the Board of Governors of, or a teacher at, any grant-aided school in Northern Ireland,

(b) relates to any person who is or has been a pupil at the school, and

(c) originated from or was supplied by or on behalf of any of the persons specified in paragraph 8,

other than information which is processed by a teacher solely for the teacher's own use.

(2) In sub-paragraph (1) "grant-aided school" has the same meaning as in the Education and Libraries (Northern Ireland) Order 1986.

8 The persons referred to in paragraph 7(1) are—

(a) a teacher at the school,

(b) an employee of an education and library board, other than such a teacher,

(c) the pupil to whom the record relates, and

(d) a parent (as defined by Article 2(2) of the Education and Libraries (Northern Ireland) Order 1986) of that pupil.

England and Wales: transitory provisions

9 (1) Until the appointed day within the meaning of section 20 of the School Standards and Framework Act 1998, this Schedule shall have effect subject to the following modifications.

(2) Paragraph 3 shall have effect as if for paragraph (b) and the "and" immediately preceding it there were substituted—

"(aa) a grant-maintained school, as defined by section 183(1) of the Education Act 1996,

(ab) a grant-maintained special school, as defined by section 337(4) of that Act, and

(b) a special school, as defined by section 6(2) of that Act, which is neither a maintained special school, as defined by section 337(3) of that Act, nor a grant-maintained special school."

(3) Paragraph 4(b)(i) shall have effect as if for the words from "foundation", in the first place where it occurs, to "1998)" there were substituted "or grant-maintained school".

SCHEDULE 12

Section 68(1)(c).

ACCESSIBLE PUBLIC RECORDS

Meaning of "accessible public record"

1 For the purposes of section 68 "accessible public record" means any record which is kept by an authority specified—

(a) as respects England and Wales, in the Table in paragraph 2,

(b) as respects Scotland, in the Table in paragraph 4, or

(c) as respects Northern Ireland, in the Table in paragraph 6,

and is a record of information of a description specified in that Table in relation to that authority.

Housing and social services records: England and Wales

2 The following is the Table referred to in paragraph 1(a).

TABLE OF AUTHORITIES AND INFORMATION

The authorities	*The accessible information*
Housing Act local authority.	Information held for the purpose of any of the authority's tenancies.
Local social services authority.	Information held for any purpose of the authority's social services functions.

3 (1) The following provisions apply for the interpretation of the Table in paragraph 2.

(2) Any authority which, by virtue of section 4(e) of the Housing Act 1985, is a local authority for the purpose of any provision of that Act is a "Housing Act local

authority" for the purposes of this Schedule, and so is any housing action trust established under Part III of the Housing Act 1988.

(3) Information contained in records kept by a Housing Act local authority is "held for the purpose of any of the authority's tenancies" if it is held for any purpose of the relationship of landlord and tenant of a dwelling which subsists, has subsisted or may subsist between the authority and any individual who is, has been or, as the case may be, has applied to be, a tenant of the authority.

(4) Any authority which, by virtue of section 1 or 12 of the Local Authority Social Services Act 1970, is or is treated as a local authority for the purposes of that Act is a "local social services authority" for the purposes of this Schedule; and information contained in records kept by such an authority is "held for any purpose of the authority's social services functions" if it is held for the purpose of any past, current or proposed exercise of such a function in any case.

(5) Any expression used in paragraph 2 or this paragraph and in Part II of the Housing Act 1985 or the Local Authority Social Services Act 1970 has the same meaning as in that Act.

Housing and social services records: Scotland

4 The following is the Table referred to in paragraph 1(b).

TABLE OF AUTHORITIES AND INFORMATION

The authorities	*The accessible information*
Local authority. Scottish Homes.	Information held for the purpose of any of the body's tenancies.
Social work authority.	Information held for any purpose of the authority's functions under the Social Work (Scotland) Act 1968 and the enactments referred to in section 5(1B) of that Act.

5 (1) The following provisions apply for the interpretation of the Table in paragraph 4.

(2) "Local authority" means—

(a) a council constituted under section 2 of the Local Government etc. (Scotland) Act 1994,

(b) a joint board or joint committee of two or more of those councils, or

(c) any trust under the control of such a council.

(3) Information contained in records kept by a local authority or Scottish Homes is held for the purpose of any of their tenancies if it is held for any purpose of the relationship of landlord and tenant of a dwelling-house which subsists, has subsisted or may subsist between the authority or, as the case may be, Scottish Homes and any individual who is, has been or, as the case may be, has applied to be a tenant of theirs.

(4) "Social work authority" means a local authority for the purposes of the Social Work (Scotland) Act 1968; and information contained in records kept by such an authority is held for any purpose of their functions if it is held for the purpose of any past, current or proposed exercise of such a function in any case.

Housing and social services records: Northern Ireland

6 The following is the Table referred to in paragraph 1(c).

TABLE OF AUTHORITIES AND INFORMATION

The authorities	*The accessible information*
The Northern Ireland Housing Executive.	Information held for the purpose of any of the Executive's tenancies.
A Health and Social Services Board.	Information held for the purpose of any past, current or proposed exercise by the Board of any function exercisable, by virtue of directions under Article 17(1) of the Health and Personal Social Services (Northern Ireland) Order 1972, by the Board on behalf of the Department of Health and Social Services with respect to the administration of personal social services under— (a) the Children and Young Persons Act (Northern Ireland) 1968; (b) the Health and Personal Social Services (Northern Ireland) Order 1972; (c) Article 47 of the Matrimonial Causes (Northern Ireland) Order 1978; (d) Article 11 of the Domestic Proceedings (Northern Ireland) Order 1980; (e) the Adoption (Northern Ireland) Order 1987; or (f) the Children (Northern Ireland) Order 1995.
An HSS trust	Information held for the purpose of any past, current or proposed exercise by the trust of any function exercisable, by virtue of an authorisation under Article 3(1) of the Health and Personal Social Services (Northern Ireland) Order 1994, by the trust on behalf of a Health and Social Services Board with respect to the administration of personal social services under any statutory provision mentioned in the last preceding entry.

7 (1) This paragraph applies for the interpretation of the Table in paragraph 6.

(2) Information contained in records kept by the Northern Ireland Housing Executive is "held for the purpose of any of the Executive's tenancies" if it is held for any purpose of the relationship of landlord and tenant of a dwelling which subsists, has subsisted

or may subsist between the Executive and any individual who is, has been or, as the case may be, has applied to be, a tenant of the Executive.

SCHEDULE 13

Section 72.

MODIFICATIONS OF ACT HAVING EFFECT BEFORE 24TH OCTOBER 2007

1 After section 12 there is inserted—

"12A Rights of data subjects in relation to exempt manual data

"12A "12A Rights of data subjects in relation to exempt manual data

(1) A data subject is entitled at any time by notice in writing—

(a) to require the data controller to rectify, block, erase or destroy exempt manual data which are inaccurate or incomplete, or

(b) to require the data controller to cease holding exempt manual data in a way incompatible with the legitimate purposes pursued by the data controller.

(2) A notice under subsection (1)(a) or (b) must state the data subject's reasons for believing that the data are inaccurate or incomplete or, as the case may be, his reasons for believing that they are held in a way incompatible with the legitimate purposes pursued by the data controller.

(3) If the court is satisfied, on the application of any person who has given a notice under subsection (1) which appears to the court to be justified (or to be justified to any extent) that the data controller in question has failed to comply with the notice, the court may order him to take such steps for complying with the notice (or for complying with it to that extent) as the court thinks fit.

(4) In this section "exempt manual data" means—

(a) in relation to the first transitional period, as defined by paragraph 1(2) of Schedule 8, data to which paragraph 3 or 4 of that Schedule applies, and

(b) in relation to the second transitional period, as so defined, data to which paragraph 14 of that Schedule applies.

(5) For the purposes of this section personal data are incomplete if, and only if, the data, although not inaccurate, are such that their incompleteness would constitute a contravention of the third or fourth data protection principles, if those principles applied to the data."

2 In section 32—

(a) in subsection (2) after "section 12" there is inserted—

"(dd) section 12A,", and

(b) in subsection (4) after "12(8)" there is inserted ", 12A(3)".

3 In section 34 for "section 14(1) to (3)" there is substituted "sections 12A and 14(1) to (3)."

4 In section 53(1) after "12(8)" there is inserted ", 12A(3)".

5 In paragraph 8 of Part II of Schedule 1, the word "or" at the end of paragraph (c) is omitted and after paragraph (d) there is inserted "or

(e) he contravenes section 12A by failing to comply with a notice given under subsection (1) of that section to the extent that the notice is justified."

SCHEDULE 14

Section 73.

Transitional provisions and savings

Interpretation

1 In this Schedule—

"the 1984 Act" means the Data Protection Act 1984;

"the old principles" means the data protection principles within the meaning of the 1984 Act;

"the new principles" means the data protection principles within the meaning of this Act.

Effect of registration under Part II of 1984 Act

2 (1) Subject to sub-paragraphs (4) and (5) any person who, immediately before the commencement of Part III of this Act—

(a) is registered as a data user under Part II of the 1984 Act, or

(b) is treated by virtue of section 7(6) of the 1984 Act as so registered,

is exempt from section 17(1) of this Act until the end of the registration period or, if earlier, 24th October 2001.

(2) In sub-paragraph (1) "the registration period", in relation to a person, means—

(a) where there is a single entry in respect of that person as a data user, the period at the end of which, if section 8 of the 1984 Act had remained in force, that entry would have fallen to be removed unless renewed, and

(b) where there are two or more entries in respect of that person as a data user, the period at the end of which, if that section had remained in force, the last of those entries to expire would have fallen to be removed unless renewed.

(3) Any application for registration as a data user under Part II of the 1984 Act which is received by the Commissioner before the commencement of Part III of this Act (including any appeal against a refusal of registration) shall be determined in accordance with the old principles and the provisions of the 1984 Act.

(4) If a person falling within paragraph (b) of sub-paragraph (1) receives a notification under section 7(1) of the 1984 Act of the refusal of his application, sub-paragraph (1) shall cease to apply to him—

(a) if no appeal is brought, at the end of the period within which an appeal can be brought against the refusal, or

(b) on the withdrawal or dismissal of the appeal.

(5) If a data controller gives a notification under section 18(1) at a time when he is exempt from section 17(1) by virtue of sub-paragraph (1), he shall cease to be so exempt.

(6) The Commissioner shall include in the register maintained under section 19 an entry in respect of each person who is exempt from section 17(1) by virtue of sub-paragraph (1); and each entry shall consist of the particulars which, immediately before the commencement of Part III of this Act, were included (or treated as included) in respect of that person in the register maintained under section 4 of the 1984 Act.

(7) Notification regulations under Part III of this Act may make provision modifying the duty referred to in section 20(1) in its application to any person in respect of whom an entry in the register maintained under section 19 has been made under sub-paragraph (6).

(8) Notification regulations under Part III of this Act may make further transitional provision in connection with the substitution of Part III of this Act for Part II of the 1984 Act (registration), including provision modifying the application of provisions of Part III in transitional cases.

Rights of data subjects

3 (1) The repeal of section 21 of the 1984 Act (right of access to personal data) does not affect the application of that section in any case in which the request (together with the information referred to in paragraph (a) of subsection (4) of that section and, in a case where it is required, the consent referred to in paragraph (b) of that subsection) was received before the day on which the repeal comes into force.

(2) Sub-paragraph (1) does not apply where the request is made by reference to this Act.

(3) Any fee paid for the purposes of section 21 of the 1984 Act before the commencement of section 7 in a case not falling within sub-paragraph (1) shall be taken to have been paid for the purposes of section 7.

4 The repeal of section 22 of the 1984 Act (compensation for inaccuracy) and the repeal of section 23 of that Act (compensation for loss or unauthorised disclosure) do not affect the application of those sections in relation to damage or distress suffered at any time by reason of anything done or omitted to be done before the commencement of the repeals.

5 The repeal of section 24 of the 1984 Act (rectification and erasure) does not affect any case in which the application to the court was made before the day on which the repeal comes into force.

6 Subsection (3)(b) of section 14 does not apply where the rectification, blocking, erasure or destruction occurred before the commencement of that section.

Enforcement and transfer prohibition notices served under Part V of 1984 Act

7 (1) If, immediately before the commencement of section 40—

(a) an enforcement notice under section 10 of the 1984 Act has effect, and

(b) either the time for appealing against the notice has expired or any appeal has been determined, then, after that commencement, to the extent mentioned in sub-paragraph (3), the notice shall have effect for the purposes of sections 41 and 47 as if it were an enforcement notice under section 40.

(2) Where an enforcement notice has been served under section 10 of the 1984 Act before the commencement of section 40 and immediately before that commencement either—

(a) the time for appealing against the notice has not expired, or

(b) an appeal has not been determined,

the appeal shall be determined in accordance with the provisions of the 1984 Act and the old principles and, unless the notice is quashed on appeal, to the extent mentioned in sub-paragraph (3) the notice shall have effect for the purposes of sections 41 and 47 as if it were an enforcement notice under section 40.

(3) An enforcement notice under section 10 of the 1984 Act has the effect described in sub-paragraph (1) or (2) only to the extent that the steps specified in the notice for complying with the old principle or principles in question are steps which the data controller could be required by an enforcement notice under section 40 to take for complying with the new principles or any of them.

8 (1) If, immediately before the commencement of section 40—

(a) a transfer prohibition notice under section 12 of the 1984 Act has effect, and

(b) either the time for appealing against the notice has expired or any appeal has been determined,

then, on and after that commencement, to the extent specified in sub-paragraph (3), the notice shall have effect for the purposes of sections 41 and 47 as if it were an enforcement notice under section 40.

(2) Where a transfer prohibition notice has been served under section 12 of the 1984 Act and immediately before the commencement of section 40 either—

(a) the time for appealing against the notice has not expired, or

(b) an appeal has not been determined,

the appeal shall be determined in accordance with the provisions of the 1984 Act and the old principles and, unless the notice is quashed on appeal, to the extent mentioned in sub-paragraph (3) the notice shall have effect for the purposes of sections 41 and 47 as if it were an enforcement notice under section 40.

(3) A transfer prohibition notice under section 12 of the 1984 Act has the effect described in sub-paragraph (1) or (2) only to the extent that the prohibition imposed by the notice is one which could be imposed by an enforcement notice under section 40 for complying with the new principles or any of them.

Notices under new law relating to matters in relation to which 1984 Act had effect

9 The Commissioner may serve an enforcement notice under section 40 on or after the day on which that section comes into force if he is satisfied that, before that day, the data controller contravened the old principles by reason of any act or omission which would also have constituted a contravention of the new principles if they had applied before that day.

10 Subsection (5)(b) of section 40 does not apply where the rectification, blocking, erasure or destruction occurred before the commencement of that section.

11 The Commissioner may serve an information notice under section 43 on or after the day on which that section comes into force if he has reasonable grounds for suspecting that, before that day, the data controller contravened the old principles by reason of any act or omission which would also have constituted a contravention of the new principles if they had applied before that day.

12 Where by virtue of paragraph 11 an information notice is served on the basis of anything done or omitted to be done before the day on which section 43 comes into force, subsection (2)(b) of that section shall have effect as if the reference to the data controller having complied, or complying, with the new principles were a reference to the data controller having contravened the old principles by reason of any such act or omission as is mentioned in paragraph 11.

Self-incrimination, etc.

13 (1) In section 43(8), section 44(9) and paragraph 11 of Schedule 7, any reference to an offence under this Act includes a reference to an offence under the 1984 Act.

(2) In section 34(9) of the 1984 Act, any reference to an offence under that Act includes a reference to an offence under this Act.

Warrants issued under 1984 Act

14 The repeal of Schedule 4 to the 1984 Act does not affect the application of that Schedule in any case where a warrant was issued under that Schedule before the commencement of the repeal.

Complaints under section 36(2) of 1984 Act and requests for assessment under section 42

15 The repeal of section 36(2) of the 1984 Act does not affect the application of that provision in any case where the complaint was received by the Commissioner before the commencement of the repeal.

16 In dealing with a complaint under section 36(2) of the 1984 Act or a request for an assessment under section 42 of this Act, the Commissioner shall have regard to the provisions from time to time applicable to the processing, and accordingly—

(a) in section 36(2) of the 1984 Act, the reference to the old principles and the provisions of that Act includes, in relation to any time when the new principles and the provisions of this Act have effect, those principles and provisions, and

(b) in section 42 of this Act, the reference to the provisions of this Act includes, in relation to any time when the old principles and the provisions of the 1984 Act had effect, those principles and provisions.

Applications under Access to Health Records Act 1990 or corresponding Northern Ireland legislation

17 (1) The repeal of any provision of the Access to Health Records Act 1990 does not affect—

(a) the application of section 3 or 6 of that Act in any case in which the application under that section was received before the day on which the repeal comes into force, or

(b) the application of section 8 of that Act in any case in which the application to the court was made before the day on which the repeal comes into force.

(2) Sub-paragraph (1)(a) does not apply in relation to an application for access to information which was made by reference to this Act.

18 (1) The revocation of any provision of the Access to Health Records (Northern Ireland) Order 1993 does not affect—

(a) the application of Article 5 or 8 of that Order in any case in which the application under that Article was received before the day on which the repeal comes into force, or

(b) the application of Article 10 of that Order in any case in which the application to the court was made before the day on which the repeal comes into force.

(2) Sub-paragraph (1)(a) does not apply in relation to an application for access to information which was made by reference to this Act.

Applications under regulations under Access to Personal Files Act 1987 or corresponding Northern Ireland legislation

19 (1) The repeal of the personal files enactments does not affect the application of regulations under those enactments in relation to—

(a) any request for information,

(b) any application for rectification or erasure, or

(c) any application for review of a decision,

which was made before the day on which the repeal comes into force.

(2) Sub-paragraph (1)(a) does not apply in relation to a request for information which was made by reference to this Act.

(3) In sub-paragraph (1) "the personal files enactments" means—

(a) in relation to Great Britain, the Access to Personal Files Act 1987, and

(b) in relation to Northern Ireland, Part II of the Access to Personal Files and Medical Reports (Northern Ireland) Order 1991.

Applications under section 158 of Consumer Credit Act 1974

20 Section 62 does not affect the application of section 158 of the Consumer Credit Act 1974 in any case where the request was received before the commencement of section 62, unless the request is made by reference to this Act.

SCHEDULE 15

Section 74(1).

MINOR AND CONSEQUENTIAL AMENDMENTS

Public Records Act 1958 (c. 51)

1 (1) In Part II of the Table in paragraph 3 of Schedule 1 to the Public Records Act 1958 (definition of public records) for "the Data Protection Registrar" there is substituted "the Data Protection Commissioner".

(2) That Schedule shall continue to have effect with the following amendment (originally made by paragraph 14 of Schedule 2 to the Data Protection Act 1984).

(3) After paragraph 4(1)(n) there is inserted—

"(nn) records of the Data Protection Tribunal".

Parliamentary Commissioner Act 1967 (c. 13)

2 In Schedule 2 to the Parliamentary Commissioner Act 1967 (departments etc. subject to investigation) for "Data Protection Registrar" there is substituted "Data Protection Commissioner".

3 In Schedule 4 to that Act (tribunals exercising administrative functions), in the entry relating to the Data Protection Tribunal, for "section 3 of the Data Protection Act 1984" there is substituted "section 6 of the Data Protection Act 1998".

Superannuation Act 1972 (c. 11)

4 In Schedule 1 to the Superannuation Act 1972, for "Data Protection Registrar" there is substituted "Data Protection Commissioner".

House of Commons Disqualification Act 1975 (c. 24)

5 (1) Part II of Schedule 1 to the House of Commons Disqualification Act 1975 (bodies whose members are disqualified) shall continue to include the entry "The Data Protection Tribunal" (originally inserted by paragraph 12(1) of Schedule 2 to the Data Protection Act 1984).

(2) In Part III of that Schedule (disqualifying offices) for "The Data Protection Registrar" there is substituted "The Data Protection Commissioner".

Northern Ireland Assembly Disqualification Act 1975 (c. 25)

6 (1) Part II of Schedule 1 to the Northern Ireland Assembly Disqualification Act 1975 (bodies whose members are disqualified) shall continue to include the entry "The Data Protection Tribunal" (originally inserted by paragraph 12(3) of Schedule 2 to the Data Protection Act 1984).

(2) In Part III of that Schedule (disqualifying offices) for "The Data Protection Registrar" there is substituted "The Data Protection Commissioner".

Representation of the People Act 1983 (c. 2)

7 In Schedule 2 of the Representation of the People Act 1983 (provisions which may be included in regulations as to registration etc), in paragraph 11A(2)—

(a) for "data user" there is substituted "data controller", and

(b) for "the Data Protection Act 1984" there is substituted "the Data Protection Act 1998".

Access to Medical Reports Act 1988 (c. 28)

8 In section 2(1) of the Access to Medical Reports Act 1988 (interpretation), in the definition of "health professional", for "the Data Protection (Subject Access Modification) Order 1987" there is substituted "the Data Protection Act 1998".

Football Spectators Act 1989 (c. 37)

9 (1) Section 5 of the Football Spectators Act 1989 (national membership scheme: contents and penalties) is amended as follows.

(2) In subsection (5), for "paragraph 1(2) of Part II of Schedule 1 to the Data Protection Act 1984" there is substituted "paragraph 1(2) of Part II of Schedule 1 to the Data Protection Act 1998".

(3) In subsection (6), for "section 28(1) and (2) of the Data Protection Act 1984" there is substituted "section 29(1) and (2) of the Data Protection Act 1998".

Education (Student Loans) Act 1990 (c. 6)

10 Schedule 2 to the Education (Student Loans) Act 1990 (loans for students) so far as that Schedule continues in force shall have effect as if the reference in paragraph 4(2) to the Data Protection Act 1984 were a reference to this Act.

Access to Health Records Act 1990 (c. 23)

11 For section 2 of the Access to Health Records Act 1990 there is substituted—

"2 Health professionals

"2 **"2 Health professionals**

In this Act "health professional" has the same meaning as in the Data Protection Act 1998."

12 In section 3(4) of that Act (cases where fee may be required) in paragraph (a), for "the maximum prescribed under section 21 of the Data Protection Act 1984" there is substituted "such maximum as may be prescribed for the purposes of this section by regulations under section 7 of the Data Protection Act 1998".

13 In section 5(3) of that Act (cases where right of access may be partially excluded) for the words from the beginning to "record" in the first place where it occurs there is substituted "Access shall not be given under section 3(2) to any part of a health record".

Access to Personal Files and Medical Reports (Northern Ireland) Order 1991 (1991/1707 (N.I. 14))

14 In Article 4 of the Access to Personal Files and Medical Reports (Northern Ireland) Order 1991 (obligation to give access), in paragraph (2) (exclusion of information to which individual entitled under section 21 of the Data Protection Act 1984) for "section 21 of the Data Protection Act 1984" there is substituted "section 7 of the Data Protection Act 1998".

15 In Article 6(1) of that Order (interpretation), in the definition of "health professional", for "the Data Protection (Subject Access Modification) (Health) Order 1987" there is substituted "the Data Protection Act 1998".

Tribunals and Inquiries Act 1992 (c. 53)

16 In Part 1 of Schedule 1 to the Tribunals and Inquiries Act 1992 (tribunals under direct supervision of Council on Tribunals), for paragraph 14 there is substituted—

"Data protection	14. (a) The Data Protection Commissioner appointed under section 6 of the Data Protection Act 1998; (b) the Data Protection Tribunal constituted under that section, in respect of its jurisdiction under section 48 of that Act."

Access to Health Records (Northern Ireland) Order 1993 (1993/1250 (N.I. 4))

17 For paragraphs (1) and (2) of Article 4 of the Access to Health Records (Northern Ireland) Order 1993 there is substituted—

"(1) In this Order "health professional" has the same meaning as in the Data Protection Act 1998."

18 In Article 5(4) of that Order (cases where fee may be required) in sub-paragraph (a), for "the maximum prescribed under section 21 of the Data Protection Act 1984" there is substituted "such maximum as may be prescribed for the purposes of this Article by regulations under section 7 of the Data Protection Act 1998".

19 In Article 7 of that Order (cases where right of access may be partially excluded) for the words from the beginning to "record" in the first place where it occurs there is substituted "Access shall not be given under Article 5(2) to any part of a health record".

SCHEDULE 16

Section 74(2).

Repeals and Revocations

Part I

Repeals

Chapter	*Short title*	*Extent of repeal*
1984 c. 35.	The Data Protection Act 1984.	The whole Act.

Chapter	Short title	Extent of repeal
1986 c. 60.	The Financial Services Act 1986.	Section 190.
1987 c. 37.	The Access to Personal Files Act 1987.	The whole Act.
1988 c. 40.	The Education Reform Act 1988.	Section 223.
1988 c. 50.	The Housing Act 1988.	In Schedule 17, paragraph 80.
1990 c. 23.	The Access to Health Records Act 1990.	In section 1(1), the words from "but does not" to the end.
		In section 3, subsection (1)(a) to (e) and, in subsection (6)(a), the words "in the case of an application made otherwise than by the patient".
		Section 4(1) and (2).
		In section 5(1)(a)(i), the words "of the patient or" and the word "other".
		In section 10, in subsection (2) the words "or orders" and in subsection (3) the words "or an order under section 2(3) above".
		In section 11, the definitions of "child" and "parental responsibility".
1990 c. 37.	The Human Fertilisation and Embryology Act 1990.	Section 33(8).
1990 c. 41.	The Courts and Legal Services Act 1990.	In Schedule 10, paragraph 58.
1992 c. 13.	The Further and Higher Education Act 1992.	Section 86.
1992 c. 37.	The Further and Higher Education (Scotland) Act 1992.	Section 59.
1993 c. 8.	The Judicial Pensions and Retirement Act 1993.	In Schedule 6, paragraph 50.
1993 c. 10.	The Charities Act 1993.	Section 12.
1993 c. 21.	The Osteopaths Act 1993.	Section 38.
1994 c. 17.	The Chiropractors Act 1994.	Section 38.

Chapter	*Short title*	*Extent of repeal*
1994 c. 19.	The Local Government (Wales) Act 1994.	In Schedule 13, paragraph 30.
1994 c. 33.	The Criminal Justice and Public Order Act 1994.	Section 161.
1994 c. 39.	The Local Government etc. (Scotland) Act 1994.	In Schedule 13, paragraph 154.

PART II

REVOCATIONS

Number	*Title*	*Extent of revocation*
S.I. 1991/1142.	The Data Protection Registration Fee Order 1991.	The whole Order.
S.I. 1991/1707 (N.I. 14).	The Access to Personal Files and Medical Reports (Northern Ireland) Order 1991.	Part II. The Schedule.
S.I. 1992/3218.	The Banking Co-ordination (Second Council Directive) Regulations 1992.	In Schedule 10, paragraphs 15 and 40.
S.I. 1993/1250 (N.I. 4).	The Access to Health Records (Northern Ireland) Order 1993.	In Article 2(2), the definitions of "child" and "parental responsibility". In Article 3(1), the words from "but does not include" to the end. In Article 5, paragraph (1)(a) to (d) and, in paragraph (6)(a), the words "in the case of an application made otherwise than by the patient". Article 6(1) and (2). In Article 7(1)(a)(i), the words "of the patient or" and the word "other".
S.I. 1994/429 (N.I. 2).	The Health and Personal Social Services (Northern Ireland) Order 1994.	In Schedule 1, the entries relating to the Access to Personal Files and Medical Reports (Northern Ireland) Order 1991.

Number	*Title*	*Extent of revocation*
S.I. 1994/1696.	The Insurance Companies (Third Insurance Directives) Regulations 1994.	In Schedule 8, paragraph 8.
S.I. 1995/755 (N.I. 2).	The Children (Northern Ireland) Order 1995.	In Schedule 9, paragraphs 177 and 191.
S.I. 1995/3275.	The Investment Services Regulations 1995.	In Schedule 10, paragraphs 3 and 15.
S.I. 1996/2827.	The Open-Ended Investment Companies (Investment Companies with Variable Capital) Regulations 1996.	In Schedule 8, paragraphs 3 and 26.

Adapted and published by GRANGIS under the OGL Licence 3.0.

www.nationalarchives.gov.uk/doc/open-government-licence/version/3/

GRANGIS - UK PUBLISHING 2022.

Thank you for taking the time to leave us a review regarding this version

★★★★★

For further inquiries, contact us at:
www.grangis.com / contact@grangis.com

www.ingramcontent.com/pod-product-compliance
Lightning Source LLC
LaVergne TN
LVHW060213210926
848481LV00008B/2723
* 9 7 9 8 8 8 5 5 9 0 1 5 0 *